JESUS THE CHRIST

CHAPTERS FOR BIBLE TEACHERS

ED GALLAGHER

CYPRESS

Copyright © 2021 by Ed Gallagher

Catalog in Publication
Gallagher, Ed (Edmon Louis), 1979-
Jesus the Christ: chapters for Bible teachers.
p. cm.
Includes scripture index.
1. Jesus Christ. 2. Jesus Christ—Study and teaching. I. Author. II. Title.
232 DDC21
ISBN: 978-1-0879-6042-5 (pbk.) ; 978-1-0879-6043-2 (ebook).
LCCN: 2021907386

Cover designed by Brad McKinnon and Brittany Vander Maas. All rights reserved.

Scripture quoted by permission. Quotations designated (NET) are from the NET Bible® copyright ©1996, 2019 by Biblical Studies Press, L.L.C. http://netbible.com All rights reserved.

No part of this book may be reproduced in any form or by any electronic or mechanical means, including information storage and retrieval systems, without written permission from the author, except for the use of brief quotations in a book review.

For more information:
Cypress Publications
PO Box HCU
3625 Helton Drive
Florence, AL 35630
www.hcu.edu

CONTENTS

Bible Abbreviations	v
Preface	xi
1. Expectations of a Messiah	1
2. The Job Description of the Messiah	8
3. A Suffering Messiah?	18
4. The Birth of a Savior	25
5. The Kingdom of God	34
6. Subverting Expectations	40
7. Fighting God's Enemies	46
8. Jesus the Teacher	52
9. More than a Messiah	58
10. Jesus and Outsiders	65
11. The Crucifixion of Jesus	71
12. The Achievement of the Cross	77
13. At God's Right Hand	83
Bibliography	91
Scripture Index	93
Also by Ed Gallagher	109

BIBLE ABBREVIATIONS

Old Testament

Gen	Genesis
Exod	Exodus
Lev	Leviticus
Num	Numbers
Deut	Deuteronomy
Josh	Joshua
Judg	Judges
Ruth	Ruth
1–2 Sam	1–2 Samuel
1–2 Kgs	1–2 Kings
1–2 Chr	1–2 Chronicles
Ezra	Ezra
Neh	Nehemiah
Esth	Esther
Job	Job
Ps	Psalms

Prov	Proverbs
Eccl	Ecclesiastes
Song	Song of Solomon
Isa	Isaiah
Jer	Jeremiah
Lam	Lamentations
Ezek	Ezekiel
Dan	Daniel
Hos	Hosea
Joel	Joel
Amos	Amos
Obad	Obadiah
Jonah	Jonah
Mic	Micah
Nah	Nahum
Hab	Habakkuk
Zeph	Zephaniah
Hag	Haggai
Zech	Zechariah
Mal	Malachi

New Testament

Matt	Matthew
Mark	Mark
Luke	Luke
John	John
Acts	Acts
Rom	Romans
1–2 Cor	1–2 Corinthians

Gal	Galatians
Eph	Ephesians
Phil	Philippians
Col	Colossians
1–2 Thess	1–2 Thessalonains
1–2 Tim	1–2 Timothy
Titus	Titus
Phlm	Philemon
Heb	Hebrews
Jas	James
1–2 Pet	1–2 Peter
1–2–3 John	1–2–3 John
Jude	Jude
Rev	Revelation

JESUS THE CHRIST

PREFACE

Most of these chapters were written for the Sunday morning adult Bible teachers at the Sherrod Avenue Church of Christ in Florence, Alabama, in the spring of 2017. They were originally conceived as material that could be taken directly into the classroom for use by a teacher. That's the point of all the questions in bold. Under the assumption that most people appreciate it when Bible classes have plenty of participation from the audience, plenty of give-and-take, I myself strive, when I teach, to get people talking by asking questions. The questions in bold are suggestions for the types of things a teacher might ask in a class. Immediately following each bolded question is a discussion guide—which I would not necessarily call the right answer to the question but at least some points that could help teachers and students formulate a helpful way of thinking about an answer. (Did I qualify that enough?) The main point of a Bible class, I guess, is to get people talking about the Bible, and that's what these chapters are trying to encourage. Each chapter concludes with five further discussion questions, which teachers could use in a variety of ways. When I originally wrote these studies, we distributed these questions to the students a week ahead of teaching the lesson so that they could be thinking and studying about the theme before class. The teacher might want to ask these questions in class. Some of these discussion questions receive treatment in the chapter itself, but not all of them. The teacher might find it most helpful to the students if everyone in the class had a copy of this book to work through on their own, which would have the added benefit of increasing my royalties.

One potential negative is that there is not a whole lot here about how you ought to behave; some people would say there's not much application in this book. While I think it's important for people to understand how to apply the Bible to their own lives, I haven't focused on modern-day application in these studies. I have assumed as of first importance that Bible students should seek to understand Scripture with new insight, and that such understanding will lead inevitably to changed lives as people are confronted with—in the case of the present book—the person of Jesus the Christ.

The Greek word *Christos* appears 529 times in the New Testament, including every book except 3 John. The proclamation of Jesus as *Christos* is an important part of the New Testament message, but what does it mean? *Christos* is a title, not a last name. He is Jesus the *Christos*, the Christ. *Christos* means "anointed" in Greek, just as Messiah means "anointed" in Hebrew, so to call Jesus the Christ is the same as calling him the Messiah: he is Jesus the Anointed One. As we will see in the first few chapters of this book, the title Messiah or Christ connects to an Old Testament promise having to do with kingship. And so Jesus the Christ is Jesus the King. Jesus who died is Jesus who rose and ascended and now sits enthroned over his kingdom. Indeed, he died and rose so that he could become Lord of the living and the dead (Rom 14:9), and that means "we will all stand before the judgment seat of Christ" (Rom 14:10). There is at least the beginning of practical Christian application in these ideas.

You could read through this book solely for your own personal edification, but I hope you'll decide to teach this material in a Bible class or small group. Most Christians I know haven't really thought about Jesus in this way, and I think it's a pretty helpful way of approaching Jesus and an eye-opening way of approaching Scripture. For a lot of people who are familiar with what the Bible says about Jesus, these lessons may make Jesus less familiar, more strange (as he certainly was to his contemporaries), and perhaps at the same time more comprehensible. So read it and teach it to others. I think I've given you enough guidance here that you can pretty easily direct a 45-minute discussion (or possibly much longer) using these chapters. I hope you'll give it a try.

CHAPTER ONE

EXPECTATIONS OF A MESSIAH

Behold, the days are coming, declares the LORD, When I will raise up for David a righteous Branch; and He will reign as king and act wisely and do justice and righteousness in the land (Jer 23:5).

Read Matthew 16:13–23. **Do you find anything surprising about this passage?** Apparently Peter did not have the same understanding of the Christ that we moderns usually have. Peter did not anticipate Jesus's death. Even when Jesus taught his disciples repeatedly that they were on their way to Jerusalem where he would die by crucifixion (see also Matt 17:22–23; 20:17–19), they were still shocked and dismayed when it happened (Matt 26:31–35, 56, 69–75). While Jesus's death for our sins more-or-less defines what we mean when we talk about the Messiah, Peter assumed the opposite, that because Jesus was the Christ or Messiah that he would therefore not die, certainly not by crucifixion. If we are to understand why people responded to Jesus the way they did, or even why Jesus acted the way he did, we need to gain a better understanding of what Jesus's contemporaries expected of the Messiah.

What does the word *messiah* mean? It is a Hebrew word that means "anointed." It appears thirty-eight times in the Old Testament. **What sorts of people were anointed in the Old Testament?**

- Priests were anointed (see Lev 8:12), and this word (in Hebrew) refers to the priest in Leviticus (4:3, 5, 16; 6:22).
- Prophets were sometimes anointed (see 1 Kings 19:16), and *messiah* refers twice to prophets (Ps 105:15 = 1 Chron 16:22).
- Kings were anointed (see 1 Sam 10:1; 16:13), and the word *messiah* refers to the ruling king in Israel very frequently.[1] Only Daniel 9:25–26 uses the term to designate a future ruler.

When first-century Jews anticipated a Messiah, what did they expect? The Messiah was the promised Savior who would come in the line of David to rule over God's kingdom. The Old Testament does not use the word *messiah* in this way, but the idea is there, as we will see.

What does the word *Christ* mean? Christ (or *Christos*) is the Greek equivalent for the Hebrew *messiah*; they both mean "anointed." In the New Testament when we see the word Christ, we could equally well render that term as Messiah. **In the New Testament, the Christ or the Messiah is presented as whose son?** At Matthew 22:41–46, Jesus asks this question of the Pharisees. They know the answer: David. While Jesus attempts to deepen their understanding of the Messiah by quoting Psalm 110:1, he does not deny that the Messiah is the son of David; in fact, Matthew's Gospel often presents Jesus as the son of David, starting with the very first verse (also 9:27; 15:22; 20:30–31; 21:9, 15; cf. 1:20). The crowds wonder whether Jesus could be the son of David (12:23).

The connection of the Messiah to David is integral to the entire expectation. The concept of the Messiah (not the word itself) goes back to the promise to David that his son would reign on the throne over Israel forever (2 Sam 7:12–16). Sometimes the beginning of the messianic hope is seen in other passages of the OT, such as in Genesis 3:15. But not only does this passage from Genesis not use the word *messiah*, neither did this passage (for the most part) contribute to the concepts that were bound up with that word in the minds of first-century Jews, who thought of the Messiah in terms of a king rather than in terms of a snake-crusher. That is not to say that Jesus does not ultimately fulfill Genesis 3:15, only that not everything Jesus fulfilled can properly be called "messianic." Jesus fulfilled the role of the Messiah, but he fulfilled other roles as well.[2]

Read 2 Samuel 7:12–17. **What kind of a king does this passage promise?** The immediate meaning of the promise is that David would establish a literal dynasty of sons ruling on the throne in Jerusalem. David's son Solomon would come to the throne after David dies, and Solomon would build a "house" (temple) for God (see 1 Kgs 6). When Solomon dies, his son would come to the throne, and so on. Unlike the way God treated Saul (2 Sam 7:15; see also 1 Sam 13:13–14; 15:11), God would not remove the kingdom from David's descendants because of sin, though he would punish them (see, e.g., 1 Kgs 11:9–13; 2 Kgs 8:19). These sons of David would enjoy a special relationship with God, being called metaphorically God's sons (see 1 Chron 22:10; 28:6; Ps 2). This promise to David (the Davidic Covenant) provided Israel with hope and security, as it seemed to the nation that God had promised to protect Israel by guaranteeing the continuation of their monarchy in perpetuity (see Ps 89:3–4, 20–37; and Ps 132).

After David's death, but still while his descendants were on the throne in Jerusalem, the prophets announced that the current descendants of David did not fulfill all of God's purposes. For instance, Isaiah prophesied about a future "shoot" springing up from the "stem of Jesse" (11:1). (Remember: Jesse was David's father; see 1 Sam 16.) He spoke this prophecy apparently while Ahaz was on the throne (see Isa 1:1; 7:1). **What would happen when this future son of David came to the throne?** Read Isaiah 11:1–10. There would be justice and there would be peace. Verses 6–9 describe a scene reminiscent of the Garden of Eden, with peace among animals and between animals and humans (see Hos 2:18; unlike now, as Deut 7:22 acknowledges). Isaiah 11:10 indicates that the Gentile nations would also be a part of this kingdom. (For a similar prophecy, but without mention of a king, see Isa 2:1–4 = Mic 4:1–3.) Similarly, during the last days of the kingdom of Judah, Jeremiah predicted a future "righteous Branch" for David who would "act wisely and do justice and righteousness" and save God's people (Jer 23:5–6; 33:14–17).

At the time of the exile (587 BC, about four centuries after the promise to David), when the reigning descendant of David was captured by Babylon (2 Kgs 25:7) so that there was no longer any Israelite king on the throne in Jerusalem, it is evident that Israel struggled to understand how God would fulfill his promise (see Ps 89:38–51). The prophets continued to point forward to a new David. Ezekiel assured the Jews in exile that God would gather them together and "set over them one shepherd, My servant David, and he will feed them" (Ezek 34:23–24; 37:24–25). Amos had earlier predicted the restoration of the fallen booth of David (Amos 9:11–15). After the exile, Zechariah continued to talk about the house of David (Zech 12:7–8, 10; 13:1). Israel awaited her Savior.

CONCLUSION

The promise to David that his descendant would reign over God's people forever ignited the messianic hopes of Israel and proved foundational for Jewish expectations of the Messiah. The Babylonian exile brought an end to the Davidic kingship in

Jerusalem but the prophets insisted that even the exile did not signal the termination of God's promise to David. It awaited fulfillment.

DISCUSSION QUESTIONS

1. Read Matthew 22:41–46. Jesus quotes Psalm 110:1 to establish that the Messiah (= Christ) is the Lord of David. Is Jesus denying that the Messiah is the son of David? (See Matt 1:1.) What is Jesus trying to teach the Pharisees?
2. Read Matthew 16:13–23. What does Peter think about the Messiah? Why does Peter think Jesus will not die in the way he predicted?
3. Read Genesis 3:14–19. Do you see a prediction of Jesus in verse 15? How so?
4. Read 2 Samuel 7:12–16. How does this passage relate to Solomon? See also 1 Chronicles 22:10; 28:6.
5. How does 2 Samuel 7:12–16 relate to Jesus?

ENDNOTES

1. 1 Sam 2:10, 35; 12:3, 5; 16:6; 24:6 [twice], 10; 26:9, 11, 16, 23; 2 Sam 1:14, 16; 19:21; 22:51; 23:1; Hab 3:13; Ps 2:2; 18:50; 20:6; 28:8; 84:9; 89:38, 51; 132:10, 17; Lam 4:20; 2 Chr 6:42. And of a foreign king: Isa 45:1.

2. Other Pentateuchal passages that did contribute to the developing picture of the Messiah include Genesis 49:9–12 and Numbers 24:17.

CHAPTER TWO

THE JOB DESCRIPTION OF THE MESSIAH

Ask of Me, and I will surely give the nations as Your inheritance, And the very ends of the earth as Your possession. You shall break them with a rod of iron, You shall shatter them like earthenware (Ps 2:8–9).

What did Peter expect the Messiah to do? Peter was the first one who voiced his belief that Jesus was the Messiah (Matt 16:13–23), but he did not think that Jesus would die on a cross. **So, what did he expect of the Messiah?** Peter expected the Messiah to be an earthly king. Sometimes it seems like we describe Peter's view in those terms as if it is strange that he would have expected the Messiah to be an earthly king. But, of course, any other view would have been strange. We saw in the previous chapter that God promised a king, and the most obvious way to understand the promise is in terms of an earthly king. When America holds a presidential election, no one asks whether the candidate will be an earthly president.

Jesus announced the coming of God's kingdom (Mark 1:15). **How did Peter think God's kingdom would be established?** He thought there would be fighting, bloodshed —and more Roman bloodshed than Jewish bloodshed. He seems to have thought that the moment of the arrest was the start of the battle (John 18:10; Luke 22:49–50). A few hours earlier, when Peter declared his intention to die with Jesus (Mark 14:31; Luke 22:33), he surely imagined a glorious death in the great battle. The Messiah was supposed to be the commander of armed forces.

Why would Peter and others think this way? What aspects of the Old Testament prophecies would make them think that the Messiah would fight a war? One way of answering this question is to look at the original promise. **The Messiah would be whose son?** As we saw in the last chapter, the Messiah is the son of David (Matt 1:1). It was David who received the initial promise of an eternal throne (2 Sam 7:12–16). This connection to David probably created the expectation that the Messiah would be just like David, a new David.

What was David like? There are two different ways of thinking about David. On the one hand, David was a spiritual giant, a "man after God's own heart" (1 Sam 13:14; Acts 13:22), the writer of the Psalms. With his harp he soothed people's spirits (1 Sam 16:23). We imagine him gently tending sheep, or gently plucking harp strings looking toward heaven, or both.

The other biblical image of David is more violent, militaristic. While still a young man, David represented his nation in battle against a Philistine giant, proving himself braver than all the Israelite warriors and King Saul (1 Sam 17). This young man cut off Goliath's head with the giant's own sword and presented it to Saul (17:51, 54, 57). Previously David had killed wild animals that threatened his sheep (17:34–36). Soon, David found such success in battle that a song credited him with having slain tens of thousands (18:5–7). After he became king, he often led his army in battle, never losing an engagement (2 Sam 8). David could be ruthless in the way he treated prisoners (8:2), just as he was in the matter of Uriah, his faithful servant whose death he arranged (11:14–17). We remember that David, though a man after God's own heart (13:14), was forbidden by God from building the temple because he had shed much blood (1 Chron 22:8; 28:3). David was a warrior king; many Jews hoped the son of David would also be a warrior king. Clearly this was the image that Peter had in his head.

Certain predictions about the coming David use military imagery, further creating the impression that the Messiah would be a warrior king like David. The passage about the "stem of Jesse" in Isaiah 11 says that this coming king "will strike the earth with the rod of His mouth, and with the breath of His lips He will slay the wicked" (v. 4). Another example is Psalm 2, which was originally a song in celebration of God's covenant with David (2 Sam 7:12–16), but, once the monarchy had been destroyed by the exile, this psalm pointed readers forward to a new king who would "break them [= the nations] with a rod of iron, You shall shatter them like earthenware" (v. 9). We can imagine how Peter and others understood such predictions.

Daniel 2 does not mention a Messiah, or David, or a Jewish king at all, but it does look forward to the establishment of the kingdom of God: "In the days of those kings the God of heaven will set up a kingdom which will never be destroyed" (Dan 2:44). But, of course, setting up God's kingdom was the job of the Messiah, so—especially for first-century Jews like Peter—this chapter contributes toward messianic expectations. According to the story, Nebuchadnezzar, king of Babylon, dreamed about a statue made of various metals, each corresponding to a particular empire (vv. 31–43). Daniel tells Nebuchadnezzar that he himself is represented by one of the metals: "You are the head of gold" (v. 38). Within the dream, a stone "cut out without hands" crushed the statue so that the metals became like chaff, carried away by the wind (vv. 34–35). This means that God's kingdom "will crush and put an end to all these kingdoms" (v. 44). Some Jews in the first century hoped for a Messiah who would crush the pagan kingdoms of the world.

Some Jews did expect a war between faithful Jews and the world (including apostate Jews and pagans). Such a war is described in great detail in one of the Dead Sea Scrolls called the War Scroll, dating to around the time of Jesus's birth.[1] Eventually such a war did happen, which led to the destruction of the Jerusalem temple in AD 70. A couple of generations later

(132–135), a man named Simon bar Kokhba was proclaimed the Messiah and led a war against Rome, enjoying some success before suffering defeat, death, and bringing brutal Roman vengeance against his people. The first-century Jewish work called the *Psalms of Solomon* expresses a similar hope for the Messiah (see Sidebar).

SIDEBAR: THE PSALMS OF SOLOMON ON THE MESSIAH

The Psalms of Solomon is a collection of poems preserved (and perhaps written) in Greek, by a Jew in the first century. The second half of the seventeenth psalm contains a lengthy description of the Messiah and the kingdom he will inaugurate. This description gives us a good idea of what Jesus' contemporaries may have expected the Messiah to do.

Psalms of Solomon 17:21–46 (NETS translation, slightly altered)

[21] See, O Lord, and raise up for them their king, the son of David,

at the time which you chose, O God, to rule over Israel your servant.

[22] And gird him with strength to shatter in pieces unrighteous rulers,

to purify Jerusalem from nations that trample her down in destruction,

THE JOB DESCRIPTION OF THE MESSIAH 13

²³ in wisdom of righteousness, to drive out sinners from the inheritance,
to smash the arrogance of the sinner like a potter's vessel,

²⁴ to shatter all their substance with an iron rod,
to destroy the lawless nations by the word of his mouth,

²⁵ that, by his threat, nations flee from his presence,
and to reprove sinners with the thought of their hearts.

²⁶ And he shall gather a holy people whom he shall lead in righteousness,

and he shall judge the tribes of the peoplethat has been sanctified by the Lord, his God.

²⁷ And he shall not allow injustice to lodge in their midst any longer,
nor shall there dwell with them any person who knows evil; for he shall know them, that all are their God's sons.

²⁸ And he shall distribute them according to their tribes upon the land,

and no resident alien and alien shall sojourn among them any longer.

²⁹ He shall judge peoples and nations in the wisdom of his righteousness.

³⁰ And he shall have the peoples of the nations to be subject to him under his yoke,

and he shall glorify the Lord in the mark of all the earth,

and he shall purify Jerusalem in holiness as it was at the beginning

³¹ so that nations may come from the end of the earth to see his glory,

bringing as gifts her sons who are exhausted,

and to see the glory of the Lord with which God has glorified her.

³² And he shall be a righteous king, taught by God, over them,
and there shall be no injustice in his days in their midst, for all shall be holy, and their king the anointed of the Lord.

³³ For he shall not put his hope in horse and rider and bow, nor shall he multiply for himself gold and silver for war, nor shall he gather hopes from a multitude of people for the

day of war.

³⁴ The Lord himself is his king, the hope of him who is strong through hope in God,

and he shall have pity on all the nations before him in fear.

³⁵ For he shall strike the earth with the word of his mouth forever;

he shall bless the people of the Lord in wisdom with joy.

³⁶ And he himself shall be pure from sin so that he may rule a great people,

that he may rebuke rulers and remove sinners by the strength of his word.

³⁷ And he shall not weaken in his days, relying on his God; for God has made him strong in the holy spirit

and wise in the counsel of understanding with strength and

righteousness.

³⁸ And the blessing of the Lord shall be with him in strength,

and he shall not weaken.

³⁹ His hope shall be in the Lord,

and who can prevail against him?

⁴⁰ He shall be strong in his works and mighty in fear of God,

shepherding the flock of the Lord faithfully and righteously,

and he shall not let any among them become weak in their pasture.

⁴¹ And he shall lead all of them in equity,
and there shall be no arrogance among them,
that any one of them should be oppressed.

⁴² This is the majesty of the king of Israel, which God knew,

to raise him up over the house of Israel to discipline it.

⁴³ His words will be more refined than costly gold, the finest.

In the congregations he will discerningly judge the tribes of a sanctified people;

his words are as words of the holy in the midst of sanctified peoples.

⁴⁴ Happy are those who shall live in those days,
to see the good things of Israel
that God shall accomplish in the congregation of the tribes.

⁴⁵ May God hasten his pity upon Israel;
may he deliver us from the uncleanness of profane enemies.

⁴⁶ The Lord himself is our king forever and ever.

All of these clues—the image of David as a warrior, a certain way of reading some messianic predictions, the wars against Rome—suggest that some first-century Jews believed that when

God kept his promises and sent his Messiah to redeem his people (Luke 24:21), this Messiah would be a military figure who would lead his forces in a great battle against the pagan enemy (i.e., Rome). Anointed by God's Spirit (Isa 11:2), he would achieve a great victory. He would gather all the scattered tribes of Israel (Deut 30:1–5; Ezek 37:21–24) and reign from Zion (Isa 2:2–4) over a reconstituted Israelite kingdom more glorious than even David's.

CONCLUSION

According to many Jews in the first century, including those whom Jesus chose as his apostles, the Messiah's job was to imitate his father David by being a warrior king, conquering the pagan nations, establishing God's kingdom, and ruling from Zion. But this picture of the Messiah misses some crucial OT hints about messianic suffering, as we will see in the next chapter.

DISCUSSION QUESTIONS

1. If King David was a model for the Messiah (see Matt 1:1; Ezek 37:24; etc.), what might this imply about the type of king the Messiah would be? What kind of king was David? Consider the story of David and Goliath (1 Sam 17).
2. Some messianic predictions used militaristic language. If a reader believed that the Messiah

would be a great military leader, what elements in Isa 11:1–10 would feed into that belief?
3. What elements in Daniel 2 might encourage someone to believe that God's kingdom would be established through military conquest?
4. Read Ezekiel 37:15–28. What impression does this passage create about the fate of the scattered tribes of Israel at the time of the Messiah? See also Jeremiah 30:8–10.
5. Based on these passages, how would you characterize the "job description" of the Messiah, as it existed in the minds of Peter and the other apostles?

ENDNOTES

1. For more information, see http://dss.collections.imj.org.il/war.

CHAPTER THREE

A SUFFERING MESSIAH?

And He said to them, "O foolish men and slow of heart to believe in all that the prophets have spoken! Was it not necessary for the Christ to suffer these things and to enter into His glory? (Luke 24:25–26)

We saw in the previous chapter that a prominent way of envisioning the Messiah in first-century Judaism was as a military figure in the likeness of David. The apostles of Jesus, especially Peter, seem to have shared these expectations. **What are some of the reasons that Jews expected a militaristic Messiah?** There were some prophecies that lent themselves to that interpretation, and of course the connection with David also seemed to point in that direction.

Early on (before the resurrection), the apostles had a hard time with the idea that the Messiah would suffer. According to the Gospels, it was only after Peter confessed his belief that Jesus was the Messiah (Matt 16:13–20; Mark 8:27–30; Luke 9:18–23) that Jesus began to teach them that he would suffer and die in Jerusalem. (Note Matt 16:21—"from that time Jesus began ..."). **Why do you think Jesus waited until this time to reveal this idea?** It may be that he felt that the apostles never would have believed him to be the Messiah if they knew what was coming.

Mark records three occasions when Jesus taught his disciples about his coming death. The first occasion is in Caesarea Philippi immediately after Peter's confession, when Peter responded by rebuking Jesus (8:31–32). **What, do you imagine, was going on in Peter's mind? Why would he rebuke Jesus?** I suspect he was thinking: "Now, wait a second! I just said you were the Messiah, and you agreed. So you can't suffer, be rejected, and be killed. That's not the plan. That's not the job description of the Messiah." Perhaps he was also thinking that Jesus's statement about his death was some sort of test; after all, Jesus had said plenty of odd things before, which had confused the apostles (Mark 4:10–12; 5:30–31; 6:37; 7:14–19; 8:14–21). Whatever his motivation, he rebuked Jesus, who then responded to Peter with his own strong rebuke, calling him Satan and accusing him of setting his mind on human interests (like staying alive, defeating the Romans, etc.) rather than the things God is interested in (8:33). Jesus proceeded to declare that the way of the cross was not for himself alone, but for everyone who "wishes to come after me" (8:34).

The second time Jesus predicted his sufferings is at Mark 9:30–32. It seems the disciples had learned their lesson; no one rebuked him this time, but neither did they understand what he was talking about, and they were afraid to ask him about it. **What did the disciples start talking about immediately after Jesus's pronouncement?** See vv. 33–37. The disciples seem to have so missed the point of Jesus's teaching about his sacrificial death that they argued with one another about which was the greatest disciple, the exact opposite of Jesus's message.

Jesus forewarned his disciples a third time at Mark 10:32–34. Mark does not tell us how they responded this time, but the immediately following episode presents James and John asking for positions of favor within the kingdom (10:35–40), so it seems they again failed to understand the nature of God's kingdom or of Jesus's messiahship.

Jesus also hints at his impending death during the Last Supper (Mark 14:22–25). According to Luke (22:24), even at this moment the disciples still argued about which of them was greatest!

It was only after the Resurrection that the disciples were prepared to understand about a suffering Messiah. Cleopas and his companion (Luke 24:18) were still very confused (vv. 19–24) until Jesus explained how the Scriptures foretold that the Messiah's glory would only follow his suffering (vv. 25–27). Later he explained to the Eleven that the Scriptures predicted the Christ's sufferings (vv. 44–48; cf. Mark 14:21, 48–49). Peter told some Jews gathered at the temple that "God announced beforehand by the mouth of all the prophets that his Christ would suffer" (Acts 3:18). Paul also explained this concept to the Jews in Thessalonica, who were not inclined to believe that the Scriptures spoke of a suffering Messiah (Acts 17:2–3). The Apostle also told the Corinthians that a fundamental part of the Gospel that he had received and delivered to them was that the "Christ died for our sins according to the Scriptures" (1 Cor 15:3).

But which Scriptures do Jesus, Peter, and Paul have in mind? The Old Testament passage that will jump immediately to mind is Isaiah 53, with its description of a suffering servant, and the New Testament certainly presents Jesus as fulfilling this passage (Matt 8:17; Luke 22:37; John 12:38; Acts 8:32–35). This Servant would bear the sins of his people (Isa 53:6, 11–12), die (vv. 7–9, 12), and apparently rise from the dead (vv. 10–11). The problem is that this passage does not mention the Messiah, David, the kingdom of God, or any other term that obviously links this suffering to a coming king. Instead, the passage talks about a Servant. No Jewish interpretation of Isaiah 53 connects the suffering to the Messiah.[1] Nevertheless, the Servant was clearly a representative of the nation, a substitute for others, and this idea might have hinted at a messianic interpretation, because the king was also a representative for the nation. At the time of Jesus, no one seems to have made this connection, for two reasons: (1) the link between the Servant and the King was very subtle, and (2) the Messiah seemed to have a very different career (conquest) from the Servant (suffering). It was Jesus who brought these concepts together (conquest through suffering).

Other passages that Jesus and the apostles may have pointed to as forecasting the suffering of the Messiah are the lamentations in the book of Psalms. The connection to the Messiah lies in the fact that many of these psalms are attributed to David in their superscriptions. These psalms narrate suffering of the Davidic psalmist (see Ps 3, 4, 5, etc.). While they do not predict in any overt way the suffering of the Messiah, they might hint that, to the extent that the Messiah will be like David, he will suffer as David suffered. Two psalms quoted in the New Testament in this regard are Psalm 16 and Psalm 22. This latter psalm is quoted several times in the Gospel accounts of Jesus's death (Mark 15:34; John 19:24); the Gospel writers believed it predicted the Messiah's suffering.[2] Acts shows both Peter (2:25–28; cf. Ps 16:8–11) and Paul (13:35; cf. Ps 16:10) quoting Acts 16 in reference to Jesus's resurrection, which implies his prior death. While Jews were not accustomed to reading these descriptions of suffering as concerning the Messiah, both apostles insist that since David died and endured decay—something that would not happen to the speaking voice of Psalm 16—the psalm must point forward to the Messiah.

CONCLUSION

Though Jews generally, and Jesus's own disciples, maintained an image of the Messiah that left no room for suffering and death, the New Testament asserts that Jewish scripture contains such predictions. We have seen some hints of this in the Old Testament, hints that largely escaped everyone's notice until after Jesus rose from the dead.

DISCUSSION QUESTIONS

1. Read Isaiah 11:1–10. Does this text create the impression of a suffering Messiah, or does it resist that impression?
2. When Jesus explains to his disciples about his upcoming suffering, they do not understand what he is talking about (Mark 9:30–32). How does their expectation of the Messiah prevent them from comprehending a suffering Messiah?
3. Why does Jesus criticize his conversation partners in Luke 24:25–26? Which scriptures would he have explained to them as predicting a suffering Messiah?
4. Read Isaiah 53. Is this passage about the Messiah? How do you know?
5. Read Psalm 22. What connections does this psalm have with the death of Jesus (see, for example, Mark 15)?

ENDNOTES

1. The evidence is in S. R. Driver and Ad. Neubauer, *The Fifty-Third Chapter of Isaiah according to Jewish Inter-*

preters (Oxford: James Parker, 1877), which you can find online.

2. See, for instance, Holly J. Carey, *Jesus' Cry from the Cross: Towards a First-Century Understanding of the Intertextual Relationship between Psalm 22 and the Narrative of Mark's Gospel* (London: T&T Clark, 2009).

CHAPTER FOUR

THE BIRTH OF A SAVIOR

> He will be great and will be called the Son of the Most High; and the Lord God will give Him the throne of His father David; and He will reign over the house of Jacob forever, and His kingdom will have no end (Luke 1:32–33).

Which two Gospels narrate the birth of Jesus? This lesson covers the birth accounts in Matthew and Luke. Mark's Gospel starts with the preaching of John the Baptist. John begins his Gospel with a birth narrative of sorts, in which the eternal Word of God put on flesh (John 1:14).

The birth narratives of Matthew and Luke stress Jesus's descent from David. The first verse of the New Testament (in its traditional arrangement) announces the coming of the

Messiah. It does so by hearkening back to the first book of the Bible, in two ways: (1) "genealogy" translates the Greek word *genesis*, already at that time the Greek title for the first book of the Bible; and (2) using a genealogy to introduce a person is a major characteristic of Genesis (see Gen 5:1; 6:9; 10:1; 11:27). **Why would Matthew want to evoke Genesis here?** Matthew considered Jesus to be the fulfillment of the Scriptures, to represent a "reboot" for humanity, and particularly a reboot for Israel (with a focus on Abraham).

What are some interesting features about the genealogy that Matthew provides in 1:2–17? Two features that we can discuss are the inclusion of women within the genealogy and the division of the genealogy into three sets of 14 names, both unusual features for biblical genealogies. **Why does Matthew mention women?** He does not mention a mother at every generation, but only four particular mothers: Tamar (v. 3), Rahab and Ruth (v. 5), and Bathsheba (v. 6)—and, of course, a fifth, Mary. These women have at least two things in common that might have prompted Matthew to mention them. First, they are all non-Israelites: Tamar was a Canaanite woman who married Judah's sons (Gen 38); Rahab was the Canaanite who received the spies (Josh 2; 6:25); Ruth was a Moabite who married Naomi's son Mahlon (Ruth 1:4; 4:10) and later married Boaz (Ruth 4:13). The exception is Bathsheba, who was apparently from the Israelite city of Gilo (cf. 2 Sam 11:3; 23:34), but she (sorta, maybe) fits the non-Israelite pattern inasmuch as she was married to Uriah the Hittite.[1] Matthew perhaps mentions these particular women in order to highlight the worldwide significance of Jesus. Second, these four women were all involved in rather questionable activities: Tamar posed as a prostitute (or, least, appeared to be one to Judah) and conceived a child with her father-in-law (Gen 38:13–15, 24–26); Rahab was a prostitute (Josh 2:1); Ruth married Boaz after a midnight encounter at the threshing floor (Ruth 3); and Bathsheba became the mother of Solomon only after an adulterous affair with David (2 Sam 11). While most people would skip over such scandalous aspects of their ancestry, Matthew accentuates the unsavory nature of humanity that brought Jesus into the world, which this new "son of David, son of Abraham" would rectify.

Why does Matthew divide this genealogy into three sections of 14? He does not tell us. Perhaps the significance of 14 is that it is twice 7, a number for perfection or completeness. Another intriguing possibility is that we should see here an example of gematria (see Wikipedia), a type of symbolism in which each Hebrew letter represents a number (another biblical example: the number of the beast; again, see Wikipedia). If Matthew is using gematria, the number 14 could indicate David's name, which is spelled in Hebrew with three consonants (no written vowels): *daleth* (= 4), *vav* (= 6), *daleth* (= 4), so that David = 14. This use of gematria would simply be another way of indicating that Jesus is the Messiah, the promised son of David.

Luke delays his presentation of Jesus's genealogy until after Jesus's baptism (Luke 3:23–38). **What are some of the differences between the genealogy in Luke and the**

version in Matthew? Luke's is backwards, starting with Jesus and going up (or is that down?) the family tree. Luke goes back to Adam (or God), Matthew goes back to Abraham. Many names differ: each genealogy mentions a different grandfather of Jesus, and they trace the line through different sons of David (Solomon vs. Nathan, on whom see, e.g., 2 Sam 5:14). (See the Sidebar at the end of this chapter for a comparison of the genealogies.) There have been many attempts to reconcile the genealogies, going back to ancient times. Two common explanations today (see here), are that either (1) Matthew presents the paternal ancestry of Jesus while Luke presents his maternal ancestry, or vice versa; or (2) Matthew presents the official, royal (but not necessarily biological) genealogy while Luke presents the actual, biological genealogy.

Two other points on Luke's genealogy: (1) it also uses number symbolism to exalt Jesus, though here the use of symbolism is less transparent than in Matthew. Starting with Adam and counting forward, the name of Jesus is the 77th name in the list. If the number 7 represents completeness, the number 77 represents super completeness (cf. Gen 4:24; Matt 18:22 ESV or NIV). (2) Adam is described as the son of God, apparently in that he had no human father (or mother) but was a direct creation by God. In this way, Adam parallels the other, greater, Son of God, whose conception was also extra-ordinary, due completely to a divine act (Luke 1:35).

Luke connects Jesus to David in several verses (1:27, 69; 2:4, 11), and he makes it clear through the angelic annunciation to Mary (1:32–33) that this baby would fulfill the promise to David of an eternal throne (2 Sam 7; see Chapter One above).

Matthew also connects Jesus to David, not only in the genealogy, but also in the subsequent story (1:20; the quotation of Mic 5:2 in Matt 2:6 [Bethlehem!]). Old Testament kings could be described metaphorically as the "son of God" (e.g., 1 Chron 22:10; 28:6), just as all Israel could be described in those terms (Exod 4:22). This is probably what Peter meant when he described Jesus as the Messiah, the son of God (Matt 16:16). (Remember, during his time with Jesus, Peter misunderstood a great deal about the Messiah.) Through their birth narratives, both Matthew and Luke want readers to recognize that Jesus is the son of God in a different sense; he is not metaphorically God's son, like all Israelite kings were, but he is literally (is that the right word?) God's son, created by a direct action of the Holy Spirit in the womb of Mary (Luke 1:35; thus, the virginal conception), so that he could be called truly Immanuel ("God with us"; Matt 1:23).

The world-changing significance of this birth is recognized by several of the characters in the story. When the Magi approach Herod seeking the "king of the Jews" (Matt 2:2; "messiah," v. 4), Herod understands that belief that a messiah has come threatens his own power (2:16). Already before Jesus's birth, both Mary (Luke 1:46–55) and Zechariah (1:67–79) sang about things God was now accomplishing, including caring for the poor (v. 53) and saving Israel from her enemies (vv. 71, 74), traditionally understood as aspects of the Messiah's work (e.g., Isa 11:4).

Conclusion

While Mark shows that a "life of Jesus" does not need to begin with his birth, Matthew and Luke use their genealogies and birth accounts to reveal crucial details about Jesus's identity: he was the promised son of David, but much more he was the son of God in an unexpected sense.

Discussion Questions

1. What is unusual about the genealogy of Jesus as presented by Matthew 1:1–17?
2. What does the angelic announcement to Joseph in Matthew 1:18–25 reveal about the identity of the coming baby?
3. In what ways is the genealogy of Jesus as presented by Luke 3:23–38 different from the genealogy as Matthew gives it?
4. What does the angelic announcement to Mary in Luke 1:26–38 reveal about the identity of the coming baby?
5. What is the significance of the Virgin Birth in Matthew 1:18–25 and in Luke 1:26–38?

ENDNOTES

1. Or should that be Uriah the Hethite? See Bryant G. Wood, "Hittites and Hethites: A Proposed Solution to an Etymological Conundrum," *Journal of the Evangelical Theological Society* 54 (2011): 239–50. If Wood is correct that Uriah was a Hethite,

then there is nothing connecting Bathsheba to "foreign-ness" as there is for the previous three women in Matthew's genealogy of Christ.

Genealogies of Jesus

Sidebar: The Genealogies of Jesus	
Matthew 1:2–16	Luke 3:23–38
	God
	1. Adam
	2. Seth
	3. Enosh
	4. Cainan
	5. Mahalaleel
	6. Jared
	7. Enoch
	8. Methuselah
	9. Lamech
	10. Noah
	11. Shem
	12. Arphaxad
	13. Cainan
	14. Shelah
	15. Heber
	16. Peleg
	17. Reu
	18. Serug
	19. Nahor
	20. Terah
Abraham	21. Abraham
Isaac	22. Isaac
Jacob	23. Jacob

Judah m. Tamar	24. Judah
Perez	25. Perez
Hezron	26. Hezron
Ram	27. Arni (= Ram?)
	28. Admin
Amminadab	29. Amminadab
Nahshon	30. Nahson
Salmon m. Rahab	31. Salmon
Boaz m. Ruth	32. Boaz
Obed	33. Obed
Jesse	34. Jesse
David m. Bathsheba	35. David
Solomon	36. Nathan
Rehoboam	37 Mattath
Abijah	38. Menna
Asa	39. Melea
Johoshaphat	40. Eliakim
Joram	41. Jonam
Uzziah	42. Joseph
Jotham	43. Judah
Ahaz	44. Simeon
Hezekiah	45. Levi
Manasseh	46. Matthat
Amon	47. Jorim
Josiah	48. Eliezer
Jeconiah	49. Joshua
	50. Er
	51. Elmadam

THE BIRTH OF A SAVIOR 33

	52. Cosam
	53. Addi
	54. Melchi
	55. Neri
Shealtiel	56. Shealtiel
Zerubbabel	57. Zerubbabel
Abihud	58. Rhesa
Eliakim	59. Joanan
Azor	60. Joda
Zadok	61. Josech
Achim	62. Semein
Eliud	63. Mattathias
Eleazar	64. Maath
Matthan	65. Naggai
Jacob	66. Hesli
	67. Nahum
	68. Amos
	69. Mattathias
	70. Joseph
	71. Jannai
	72. Melchi
	73. Levi
	74. Matthat
	75. Eli
Joseph m. Mary	76. Joseph
Jesus	Jesus

CHAPTER FIVE

THE KINGDOM OF GOD

Now having been questioned by the Pharisees as to when the kingdom of God was coming, He answered them and said, "The kingdom of God is not coming with signs to be observed; nor will they say, 'Look, here it is!' or, 'There it is!' For behold, the kingdom of God is in your midst." (Luke 17:20–21).

What is the kingdom of God? Some people think that the kingdom of God is completely future, that Jesus will establish it at his Return. The Churches of Christ have traditionally identified the kingdom of God closely with the church.[1] **What did the contemporaries of Jesus**

think about the kingdom of God? We saw in Chapter Two that the "job description" of the Messiah was to establish God's kingdom on the model of David's kingdom. (Of course, God has always been king [cf. Ps 96:10; 97:1; etc.], but he would become king with a kingdom in a more obvious way at the coming of the Messiah and the establishment of the kingdom of God.) Many Jews in the first century hoped for the time when God would gather all the tribes of Israel together again and establish them as a strong nation under a new David as their king (a hope based on prophetic passages such as Ezek 37:15–28). They had experienced, instead, centuries of domination by foreign oppressors and progressively diminished influence and power as a nation. The memory of past glory combined with the reality of present powerlessness surely contributed to inflaming first-century Jewish hope for God to accomplish a great reversal in terms of a powerful Israelite state and the defeat of his enemies, especially the Romans.

Attentive readers can find hints of such expectations throughout the Gospels. For example, the criminal whose life was spared in place of Jesus—Barabbas—probably harbored such hopes. According to Mark 15:7, "Barabbas had been imprisoned with the insurrectionists who had committed murder in the insurrection." This insurrection had happened "in the city" (Luke 23:19), no doubt the city of Jerusalem. Since Barabbas was condemned to the fate of crucifixion by the Romans, we should imagine that the people he had murdered were Romans, perhaps soldiers. The insurrection in which he participated would have been intending to overthrow the Roman powers. This insurrection was very small scale, since we hear about it nowhere else, but it foreshadowed the rebellion a generation later that resulted in the destruction of the Jewish Temple in AD 70. This earlier rebellion in which Barabbas participated was probably something on the scale of the mob action that led to the Boston Massacre in 1770. Some Jews (Barabbas among them?) could likely have echoed Patrick Henry's famous cry, "Give me liberty or give me death!" It is plausible that Barabbas imagined that the kingdom of God would come through such violent actions, in accordance with a quite straightforward reading of prophecies such as Daniel 2 (note especially verses 34–35).

What did Jesus say about the kingdom of God? He said all kinds of things about it. His teaching primarily emphasized this topic. The first words he says in Mark's Gospel are: "The time is fulfilled and the kingdom of God is at hand; repent and believe in the gospel" (1:15). What he meant—and what his Jewish audience would have understood by this announcement—was that God was about to make good on his ancient promise to establish his kingdom through a descendant of David. The phrase "kingdom of God" then appears in Mark thirteen more times.[2]

Luke uses the phrase "kingdom of God" 32 times, and also mentions the "gospel of the kingdom" (16:16). Matthew perhaps emphasizes the coming kingdom more than any other gospel writer, since he uses the noun "kingdom" 55 times. But Matthew uses the phrase "kingdom of God" only four times (12:28; 19:24; 21:31; 21:43). Instead, he regularly employs the phrase "kingdom of heaven" (32x), clearly equivalent to "kingdom of God" (compare Matt 4:17 // Mark 1:15; or Matt

19:14 // Mark 10:14).[3] Scholars debate the reason for this change of terminology in Matthew; at any rate, since heaven is God's dwelling place, the two phrases share identical meanings (like using the term "White House" in place of the term President).

John uses the terminology of God's kingdom much less than the Synoptic Gospels, only in Jesus's conversation with Nicodemus (3:3, 5; cf. 18:36). In John, Jesus speaks more about "life" (36x) than about the kingdom. But, this Gospel, no less than the others, makes it clear that Jesus was the Messiah, whose job it was to usher in God's kingdom.[4]

The whole ministry of Jesus aimed not only at preparing people for God's kingdom but also at establishing that kingdom. **How did Jesus prepare people for the kingdom?** (Concentrating here on Matthew) He called on people to repent (Matt 4:17), just as his predecessor John had (3:2). He taught about who would be in the kingdom (5:3, 10; 18:3–4; 19:12; 21:31), and who wouldn't (5:19–20; 7:21; 8:11–12; 19:23; 21:43). He himself proclaimed the kingdom (9:35) and instructed others to do so as well (10:7; cf. Luke 9:60). He told parables explaining the nature of the kingdom (13:24, 31, 33, 44, 45, 47; 18:23; 20:1; 22:2; 25:1; etc.). He insisted that it was near (16:28), even in their midst (cf. Luke 17:21), though they might not be able to see it (cf. John 3:3). **How did he establish the kingdom during his ministry?** His teaching certainly contributed toward that. Also, he cast out demons and healed diseases, both signs of the nearness of God's kingdom (Matt. 9:35; 12:28; cf. Luke 10:9). Just as God had promised to regather all the tribes of Israel within the messianic kingdom, so the Gospel writers ensure us that Jesus gathered followers from the entire extent of David's kingdom (Matt 4:24–25), and he appointed twelve of his followers to be special envoys (apostles, cf. Mark 3:13–19), who themselves represented the regathering of the tribes (cf. Luke 22:30).

Of course, the great action whereby Jesus established the kingdom happened on the cross, the moment of his coronation (Mark 15:17), when he was publicly proclaimed "King of the Jews" (15:26). But this clearly means that Jesus was a very different type of king, different from Herod, even different from David; his kingdom would be "not of this world" (John 18:36).

CONCLUSION

After his resurrection, Jesus had been granted "all authority in heaven and on earth" (Matt 28:18). He came announcing a kingdom, and he had now ascended to his throne. But this king and his kingdom did not conform to expectations, an idea we'll explore in the next chapter.

DISCUSSION QUESTIONS

1. Reflect on God as king in the Old Testament. Look at 1 Samuel 8:7; Psalm 97:1; 98:6; Daniel 2:44. In what ways was God already king and in what ways was his kingdom future?

2. The ministry of Jesus focused on announcing the coming kingdom of God (Matt 4:17; 9:35; 10:7). What would Jesus's audience have thought about this announcement?
3. In what ways does John's ministry prepare the way for the establishment of God's kingdom? (Matt 3).
4. Jesus often casts out demons (Mark 1:21–28; 5:1–20; 9:14–29). How does these exorcisms contribute toward Jesus's kingdom announcement? (See Matt 12:28; Luke 11:20.)
5. How do Jesus's contemporaries interpret these exorcisms? See, e.g., Mark 1:27–28; Matthew 8:16; 12:22–24; cf. John 8:48–52.

ENDNOTES

1. See my chapter on this theme in *The Ekklesia of Christ*, Berean Study Series (Florence, AL: HCU Press, 2015).

2. Mark 4:11, 26, 30; 9:1, 47; 10:14–15, 23–25; 12:34; 14:25; 15:43; cf. 11:10 ("kingdom of our father David").

3. For more on this, see the opening chapter of my *The Sermon on the Mount: Explorations in Christian Practice*, Cypress Bible Study Series (Florence, AL: HCU Press, 2021).

4. Gospel passages identifying Jesus as "Christ" (= Messiah): Matt 1:1, 16, 17, 18; 11:2; 16:16, 20; 26:63–64; 27:17, 22; Mark 1:1; 8:29; 14:61–62; Luke 2:11, 26; 4:41; 9:20; 23:2; 24:26; John 1:17, 41; 11:27; 17:3; 20:31. The title "Christ" applied to Jesus is much more common in Acts and the letters.

CHAPTER SIX

SUBVERTING EXPECTATIONS

The Jews answered and said to Him, "Do we not say rightly that You are a Samaritan and have a demon?" (John 8:48)

What did Jews in the first-century expect out of the Messiah? We have seen (especially in Chapter Two) that the Messiah was supposed to establish the kingdom of God by means of force, just like David did. (Remember: "David has killed his tens of thousands," 1 Sam 18:7.) Jesus came announcing the kingdom of God (as we saw in the previous chapter), but he did not conform to the type of Messiah that was generally anticipated.

What are some ways that Jesus subverted people's expectations of a Messiah? Most obviously, people did not expect the Messiah to die (see Chapter Three). They thought he would be killing Romans rather than being killed by the Romans. Just as David had cut off the giant's head (1 Sam 17:51), some Jews probably hoped for a Messiah who would do the same thing to Herod or Caesar. Peter was ready to help (John 18:10). Jesus's combining the role of the Suffering Servant (Isa 53) with the role of the Messiah proved utterly baffling to his own disciples until after the resurrection. They failed to understand that he did not come to fight the Romans. Jesus said if his kingdom were like any other, his servants would fight (John 18:36). Nations are always established through violence. David established his kingdom through warfare (note 2 Sam 3:1; 5:6–10; 8:1–13). The Romans did too. (Consider also the American Revolution.) People thought the Messiah would as well. Jesus said that would be the case if his were a regular kingdom, but in fact his kingdom is "not of this world," and so it is established in a different way, without violence.

Some of his teaching aimed at the same theme. Jesus blessed peacemakers (Matt 5:9), not something one expects to hear from a rebel leader. He counseled his audience to turn the other cheek (v. 39) and, when forced into service, to go the extra mile (v. 41). He told them they ought to love their enemies and pray for them (v. 44). He made sacrifice the basis for his kingdom, telling any would-be follower that discipleship invariably involves cross-bearing (16:24).

Jesus routinely tried to silence talk about his own messiahship. He would tell those he had healed to be quiet (Mark 1:44;

5:43; 7:36; 8:26), often in vain. The demons announced Jesus's identity, and Jesus rebuked them for it (Mark 1:24–25, 32–33; 3:12). When Peter had confessed that Jesus was the Messiah, Jesus accepted the designation but told his disciples to keep it quiet (8:30; cf. 9:9). The major exception is the man who had the Legion, when Jesus instructed him to spread the word (Mark 5:19–20), possibly because he was in a Gentile region, not a Jewish one (note the pigs, v. 12). Jesus perhaps gave a statement of principle in this regard at Mark 4:10–12, where he explained why he used parables, so that people would have a hard time understanding him. The theme of secrecy seems to be connected to the misunderstandings about the Messiah that were prevalent among Jews at the time. Jesus did not want to encourage speculation about his political or military ambitions (a problem that would not be so great among Gentiles).

What was the relationship between Jesus and the Jewish leadership? They had a tense relationship, due mostly to Jesus's refusal to conform to their standards. The leadership expected their Messiah to uphold (their interpretation of) the Torah and to establish a kingdom "of this world." Jesus intended to do neither. We've discussed the second element. As for the first, Jesus considered the Pharisees to be blind guides (Matt 23:16) who often broke God's law to preserve their own traditions (15:1–14). When they presented correct teaching, they failed to practice it (23:2–4). He refused to grant them a sign on demand (Mark 8:11–13). (Of course, these general accusations do not apply to each individual Pharisee but to those with whom Jesus interacted and who opposed him.) Jesus said that he did not obey the Pharisaic interpretation of the Sabbath because he himself was Lord of the Sabbath

(Mark 2:28). That was something David could not say, so why would David's son be saying it? It turned out that this son of David was also David's Lord (Mark 12:35–37). Jesus also presented his own interpretations of the Torah (e.g., Matt 5:17–48) and became a recognized authority on Old Testament exegesis, sometimes correcting Pharisaic or Sadducean interpretation (Mark 10:1–12; 13:18–27).

The fact that Jesus interacted with certain "off-limits" people also shocked and angered others. Jesus attended parties thrown by tax collectors and attended by sinners (Mark 2:15–17; Luke 19:1–10). He spoke with a Samaritan woman (John 4) and once used a Samaritan as the hero in a story (Luke 10:30–37). He refused to condemn the sinful woman at Simon's house (Luke 7:36–50). He did not befriend the rich, but told one rich man to give away all his possessions (Mark 10:17–31), and he praised a poor widow's offering instead of the extravagant offerings of the rich (12:41–44).

Despite all this, the works that Jesus performed compelled people to pay attention to him. He was known widely as a healer, so that people often implored him on behalf of their sick friends or relatives (Mark 1:32–34; 2:3–4; 9:17–18), including even synagogue officials (5:22–23) and Gentiles (7:24–26; Matt 8:5–6).[1] This power astonished people (Mark 7:37), as did his authority over the demons (1:27), his power over nature (4:41), and his teaching (Matt 7:28–29)

What did people think about Jesus? Many thought he was a prophet of some sort (Mark 8:27–28; cf. 6:14–15; John 4:19; 6:14; 7:40; 9:17) or the Christ (Mark 8:29; John 1:41; 7:25–31, 41–44). Others thought he was a party animal (Matt

11:19), or a Samaritan (John 8:48), or in league with Satan (Matt 12:22–24) or possessed by a demon (John 7:20; 8:48–52; 10:20–21).

The most subversive thing about Jesus was his compassion, not the sort of thing one expected of a warrior. Certainly it is hard to imagine the messianic hopeful Simon bar Kokhba (see Wikipedia) a century later (AD 132–135) counseling his followers to be like children (Matt 18:1–4) or instructing them to invite to dinner the outcasts (Luke 14:16–24) or telling a story in which kindness expressed to "the least of these" becomes the basis for judgment (Matt 25:31–46).

Conclusion

Jesus subverted popular expectations of a Messiah in many ways, sometimes disappointing people because he refrained from taking a stronger stance against the Romans, other times angering people because he refused to bow to the religious authorities, but often amazing people with his unbelievable power and inherent authority. What Jesus offered is often not what people expected or wanted.

Discussion Questions

1. People had many different reactions to Jesus, some of them quite negative. Besides John 8:48, see also Matthew 11:19 and 12:22–24. Why did some people have such strong negative reactions to Jesus?

2. Why did the religious leadership get so angry with Jesus? See Mark 2:1–3:6; 7:1–23; 8:11–13; etc.
3. Why did Jesus sometimes tell people to keep quiet about his own identity? See Mark 1:24–25, 32–33, 44; 3:12; 5:43; 8:30; etc.
4. On the other hand, why did he instruct the man healed of the legion of demons to proclaim what God had done (Mark 5:19–20)?
5. Why did some people come to believe that Jesus was the Messiah? See John 1:41; 7:25–31, 41–44; Mark 8:29.

ENDNOTES

1. Other examples showing the fame of Jesus as a healer: Mark 1:40; 5:25–28; 6:53–57; 7:32; 8:22; 10:46–52.

CHAPTER SEVEN

FIGHTING GOD'S ENEMIES

To grant us that we, being rescued from the hand of our enemies, might serve Him without fear (Luke 1:74).

What was the common expectation of the Messiah? Jews in the first century expected a Messiah who would fight against God's enemies. **Why did they think this?** The Old Testament seems to imply (or, directly state) this idea in several prophecies (e.g., Isa 11:4; Ps 2:8–9; etc.). Since the Romans were the pagan nation in power over the Jews in the first century, they were the enemies that the Messiah was supposed to fight, as many people thought. Jesus proved to be frustratingly reticent to raise arms against the Romans or anyone else.

Though Jesus the Messiah did not fight the particular

enemies that many Jews expected, the Gospels do show that Jesus fought against God's enemies. But just as the kingdom established by Jesus was not "of this world" (John 18:36), so also the enemies that he fought were not of this world (see Eph 6:12!). On a number of occasions in John's Gospel, Jesus mentions a "ruler of this world," who has been judged (16:11) and will be cast out (12:31; cf. 14:30). It is this ruler (Satan, 13:27; the devil; 8:44; 13:2), and not the Romans, that Jesus came to battle.

In what ways did Jesus battle Satan during his ministry? There are a number of ways that we can see this battle. First of all, immediately after his baptism, Jesus went into the desert for 40 days "to be tempted by the devil" (Matt 4:1). While Mark merely alludes to this incident (Mark 1:12–13), Matthew (4:1–11) and Luke (4:1–13) record three particular temptations that the devil tried on Jesus. Each time Jesus responded by quoting Deuteronomy (8:3; 6:13, 16), resisting temptation by the power of Scripture, so that the devil finally left. This initial victory over Satan exhibits the type of warfare in which Jesus would engage, as well as his prowess in such conflicts.

The early part of Jesus's ministry was full of encounters with demons or unclean spirits (synonymous terms, as Mark 5:1–20 show). During an early visit to a synagogue in Capernaum, Jesus exorcised a demon from a man, prompting the response from the crowd, "What is this? A new teaching with authority! He commands even the unclean spirits, and they obey Him" (Mark 1:21–27). The demons recognized Jesus as having power over them (1:24; 5:7, 12). Jesus quickly became known as an exorcist (1:32–34; 7:24–30; 9:17–29), and he gave the Twelve power over the demons (3:14–15; 6:7, 13; cf. Luke 10:19). Others could expel demons by invoking the name of Jesus (Mark 9:38; but cf. Acts 19:13–17). Demons afflicted people in various ways: making a boy mute (Mark 9:17), foam at the mouth and slamming him down (9:18), convulsing a man (1:26), leading a man to hurt himself (5:5), but also giving him unusual strength (5:4), and causing this man such trouble that he withdrew from society (5:3). But Jesus overpowered the demons.

Jesus's fame as an exorcist soon led to controversy as to whether he might be using demonic power (Mark 3:22–30). We have seen that the crowd was amazed at Jesus's authority over the demons, and the suggestion that Jesus was in league with Satan also confirms how unusual was the power to cast out demons. Jesus responded by assuring the crowd that his fight against Satan certainly did not indicate an alliance with Satan. Jesus told a parable about a man entering a strong man's house and binding him in order to plunder his house (3:27), implying that Jesus's exorcisms should be interpreted as signaling the defeat of the strong man, Satan (cf. Luke 10:17–18). Indeed, the exorcisms represented the coming of the kingdom of God (Matt 12:28).

Similarly, Jesus also became famous as a healer, so much so that people quickly sought out Jesus for that very purpose (e.g., Mark 1:32–34, 40; 2:1–12; 5:25–27; 7:32; 8:22; 10:46–52), including synagogue officials (Mark 5:22–23), centurions (Matt 8:5–6), and royalty (John 4:46–47). At one point Jesus explicitly connected his healing ministry to his spiritual war by describing a sick woman as being bound by Satan (Luke 13:16). Even if we cannot apply this description to all of Jesus's patients—since Luke mentions that this particular woman had "a sickness caused by a spirit" (v. 11), which, presumably, does not apply to every sickness— Peter similarly summarizes Jesus's life by mentioning that he healed "all who were oppressed by the devil" (Acts 10:38). While we certainly cannot strictly connect sickness to sin (see John 9:1–3), we can say that sickness is an evil part of the world that will be abolished by God. In his ministry, Jesus overcame that evil.

The teachings of Jesus also served as an attack against evil forces. It is Satan's work to encourage people to treat others harshly (Matt 5:38–48) or to lust (5:27–30) or to focus on physical needs (6:25–34; 13:22), all of which Jesus taught against. It is Satan who puts evil plans into people's hearts (John 13:2). Jesus's teaching promotes resistance to the schemes of the devil, which is why the devil works to take the word away from people's hearts (Mark 4:15).

The enemies of Israel—the enemies of all humans—include sin and death. Jesus spent a lot of time defeating the former and he struck the deathblow against the latter. Gabriel told Joseph that his son would "save his people from their sins" (Matt 1:21). John the Baptist baptized people for the forgiveness of sins (Luke 3:3; cf. 1:77), thus preparing the way of the Lord. During his ministry, Jesus demonstrated his surprising authority over sin by offering forgiveness (Mark 2:1–12; Luke 7:47–49). The way Jesus secured forgiveness (the defeat of sin) is, of course, through the blood of his cross, as the Lord's Supper commemorates (Matt 26:28). This was also the means by which he conquered death and the one who held death's power (Heb 2:14). But it was impossible for death to hold Jesus, so God raised him up, "putting an end to the agony of death" (Acts 2:24), though we await the full and final defeat of this "last enemy" (1 Cor 15:26). We have assurance from Jesus that God will put all enemies under his feet (Ps 110:1; Mark 12:36).

CONCLUSION

The common expectation in the first century was that the Messiah would conquer the Romans, because they were the enemies of God. The ministry of Jesus shows us that the Romans were small potatoes in the grand scheme of things, and the Messiah had much bigger goals, much more sinister enemies to fight. He came to do battle with God's true enemies: Satan, along with sin and death. At the beginning of his ministry, Satan offered Jesus "all the kingdoms of the world and their glory" (Matt 4:8–9); by the end, Jesus's conquest over Satan gained him "all authority ... in heaven and on earth" (28:18).

DISCUSSION QUESTIONS

1. What might Zechariah have meant when he said that God was about to keep his oath to Abraham to rescue his people from their enemies? See Luke 1:67–79.

2. In what ways did Jesus do battle with Satan? See Matthew 4:1–11; 12:22–29.
3. How do healings work within Jesus's ministry and his battle with Satan? See Luke 13:16; Acts 10:38.
4. In what ways did Jesus do battle with sin? See Matthew 1:21; 26:28; Mark 2:1–12.
5. In what ways did Jesus do battle with death? See Acts 2:24; Hebrews 2:14.

CHAPTER EIGHT

JESUS THE TEACHER

> But they kept insisting, saying, "He stirs up the people, teaching all over Judea, starting from Galilee even as far as this place" (Luke 23:5).

Jesus was well-known as a teacher. People often addressed him as "Teacher" (Matt 8:19; 12:38; Mark 4:38; Luke 7:40), or, in Hebrew, "Rabbi" (John 1:38; 3:2; cf. 20:16). Sometimes he was known as "the Teacher" (John 11:28).[1] He frequently taught in synagogues (Matt 4:23; 9:35; 13:54) or at the temple (Matt 21:23; John 7:28) or on the seashore (Mark 2:13) or in villages (Mark 6:6) or from a boat (Luke 5:3) or in a house (Luke 5:17; cf. Mark 2:1-2). The crowds considered his teaching remarkable because of its authority, an authority evident in the way he presented the message (Matt 7:28-29; 22:33; Mark 11:18), but also an authority manifest in his power over demons (Mark 1:27). It was his teaching that got him in trouble (Luke 23:5).

What was Jesus trying to accomplish through his teaching? The core of Jesus's message concerned the impending arrival of the kingdom of God: "The time is fulfilled, and the kingdom of God is at hand; repent and believe in the gospel" (Mark 1:15). His teaching was aimed at preparing people for life within God's kingdom. **How does the Sermon on the Mount prepare people for the kingdom of God?** The Sermon on the Mount—the first of five major blocks of teaching in Matthew's Gospel[2]—encourages people to reorient their lives away from "normal" standards of living and toward God's standards. (This is the practical outworking of how to "repent" [Matt 4:17], parallel to John the Baptist's exposition of the same theme in Luke 3:7–18.) Jesus assures people that the truly blessed are not the rich and powerful but the poor in spirit, the peacemakers, the gentle and merciful, those persecuted for righteousness sake (Matt 5:3–12). Rather than getting as close to sin as possible without crossing the line, people should live according to the spirit of the command: if the command is not to murder, then you should not even hate (5:21–26); if the command is not to commit adultery, then you should not even lust (5:27–30). If people want to prepare themselves for the inbreaking of God's kingdom, they will refrain from personal vengeance but instead treat even their enemies with respect and love (5:38–48). The rest of the sermon continues the same themes: making your religion truly personal so that you pray and fast, but not for show (6:1–18), and you do not love money (6:19–24), that you trust God to provide for you (6:25–34), that you stop hypocritically judging others (7:1–6), that you treat others how you want to be treated (7:12). None of these teachings would be the expected points of emphasis for Israel's Messiah, but as we saw in Chapter Six, Jesus is not Israel's expected Messiah, he is Israel's unexpected Messiah. And his Sermon on the Mount reveals the unexpected ethical dimension to living within God's kingdom.

One of the things that amazed the crowds but also frustrated Jesus's opponents was the way he interpreted Scripture. He challenged his opponents to "go and learn" about Scripture (Matt 9:13, citing Hos 6:6). He criticized the Sadducees for their ignorance of Scripture (Matt 22:29). When the Pharisees rebuked Jesus for breaking a tradition (15:2), he responded by accusing them of breaking the Ten Commandments (15:3–4), a much more serious charge. **In what way were the Pharisees breaking a commandment in this passage?** Jesus says they were teaching that an offering made to God (he uses the Hebrew word *korban*) superseded any other purpose for the money, including helping aged parents. Jesus sees this practice as a blatant violation of the fifth commandment.

Jesus often taught in parables (in the Synoptic Gospels, not in John). **Why would Jesus teach in parables?** The parables helped some people understand the nature of God's kingdom, but they also obscured the message from others. These two goals of parables are mentioned in Mark 4, where Jesus says that his stories hide "the mystery of the kingdom of God" from those who are not able to hear (vv. 11–12), but Mark explains that Jesus used parables to teach people "as far as they were able to hear it" while "explaining everything privately to his own disciples" (vv. 33–34). The parables illustrate life in the kingdom of God.

Read Matthew 13:44–50. **What do these parables say about the kingdom of God?** All three parables seem to illustrate the hiddenness of God's kingdom (cf. Luke 17:20–21). In the first two, the kingdom is worth much, one's whole livelihood (cf. Matt 16:24–26), but it still produces incredible joy. The third parable is reminiscent of the Parable of the Tares (Matt 13:24–30, 36–43), explaining that even within the kingdom the righteous and the wicked still abide together until "the end of the age" when the wicked are culled and punished. This parable perhaps helps explain why the kingdom Jesus preached does not look exactly like certain prophecies about the kingdom such as Isaiah 11:4, in which the wicked are punished at the coming of the Messiah.

Read Mark 12:1–11. **What does this parable say about the kingdom of God?** This parable is a fairly transparent story about the history of Israel culminating in God's rejection and punishment of the Jerusalem religious leadership. Indeed, the point of this parable was so clear that even Jesus's opponents understood it (v. 12). Those who had been in control of God's vineyard (the kingdom) would be cast out because of their obstinance and wickedness, not to mention their stupidity in thinking that murdering the heir would result in their inheriting the vineyard. Jesus says (vv. 10–11) that they should have understood this principle from Psalm 118:22, a psalm connected in Jewish tradition (in which it is part of the *Hallel*; see Wikipedia) closely with the Passover celebration which they were about to observe. The parable says that things are about to change, a reversal is coming.

Read the parable of the rich man and Lazarus (Luke 16:19–31). **What does this parable say about the kingdom of God?** Like much of Jesus's teaching, and demonstrated by much of his own life, this parable demands that Jesus's followers open their eyes and get involved in the problems of the world, refusing to say "that's not my problem."

CONCLUSION

We have barely scratched the surface of Jesus's teaching, and we have not even taken a glance at John's Gospel, which contains no parables but more exalted (and, sometimes, confusing) teaching from Jesus. The subversive nature of Jesus's teaching—particularly the way he exposed hypocrisy and predicted a great reversal in which those in power would be brought low—angered his opponents and compelled them to plan his death. For followers of Jesus, his teaching provides a picture of life in the kingdom, a lifestyle for us to adopt.

DISCUSSION QUESTIONS

1. What was the main message of Jesus's teaching? See

Mark 1:15; Matthew 5:3; etc.

2. How does the Sermon on the Mount (Matt 5–7) relate to Jesus's proclamation of the kingdom of God? What is Jesus teaching about the kingdom in this sermon?
3. Why do you think the crowds were so amazed at Jesus's teaching (Matt 7:28–29; 22:33)?
4. Why did Jesus teach in parables? See Mark 4:10–12, 33–34; and compare Matthew 13:10–17.
5. What was Jesus trying to say in the Parable of the Tenants (Mark 12:1–11)? Why did this parable enrage his opponents (v. 12)?

ENDNOTES

1. However, Jesus is never called "teacher" in Acts or the Letters, only in the Gospels.
2. Each of these five blocks of teaching concludes with some variation of the expression, "When Jesus had finished these words..." (Matt 7:28; 11:1; 13:53; 19:1; 26:1).

CHAPTER NINE

MORE THAN A MESSIAH

And they were filled with great fear and said to one another, "Who then is this, that even the wind and the sea obey him?" (Mark 4:41)

Read Mark 12:35–37. **What point is Jesus trying to make?** Jesus does not deny that the Messiah is the son of David. He accepts the title Messiah (see Mark 8:27–30 // Matt 16:13–20; Mark 14:61–62) and the title son of David (Mark 10:46–52; cf. Matt 1:1; Luke 1:32). Rather, he is pushing his audience to consider whether the Messiah might be more than David's son, whether he could be David's lord, as Psalm 110:1 indicates. Within the story Mark is telling, this incident is just one of several indications that Jesus the Christ is not the Christ that we expected (see Chapter Six).

The first eight chapters of Mark's narrative build up to

Peter's confession of Jesus as Christ (= Messiah; 8:27–30). Readers were already assured that this title belonged to Jesus (Mark 1:1), but the next time (after 1:1) the word "Christ" appears in Mark's Gospel is on the lips of Peter at 8:29. Jesus's words and actions up to that point had been designed, in part, to convince his disciples that he was indeed the Christ. They had been a little slow on the uptake (cf. 8:14–21; 6:52; compare 8:18 with 4:11–12), but it came together at Caesarea Philippi (8:27–30). The last eight chapters of Mark explain the type of Messiah Jesus was, starting with the assurance that this Messiah would die on a cross (8:31), an idea unacceptable to Peter (8:32). But there is also emphasis on the exalted nature of Jesus. In fact, the two ideas go hand-in-hand: suffering leads to exaltation, and those wishing to be first must become slaves (10:44).

In what ways do the Gospels portray Jesus as divine? John's Gospel clearly reveals Jesus as the embodiment of God. This idea is clear not only from John's prologue (1:1–18) but also from the continuing story in which Jesus says things like "I and the Father are one" (10:30) or "before Abraham was born, I am" (8:58). Jesus's audience understood that he claimed divine status for himself (5:18). Jesus is actually called "God" three times in John's Gospel (1:1, 18; 20:28).[1] The other Gospels are not quite so obvious in the way that they present the divinity of Jesus, but even Mark (the briefest Gospel with the least emphasis on Jesus's exalted status) persistently hints at Jesus's divinity. The very beginning of the Gospel quotes Isaiah 40:3, "Make ready the way of the Lord." In its Old Testament context, the Lord in this verse is Yahweh, the God of Israel, but Mark applies the verse to Jesus.[2]

Whereas people seemed uncertain of Jesus's identity, the demons knew exactly who he was (1:24; 3:11; 5:7). The scribes believed that only God could forgive sins (2:7), but Jesus claimed that authority for himself (2:5, 10). God instituted the Sabbath (Exod 20:4–11), but Jesus declared himself Lord of the Sabbath (2:28). Jesus commanded the wind and the sea (4:39–41), a characteristic of God in the Old Testament (Ps 107:29; cf. Ps 65:7; 89:9; Job 38:8–11).

Immediately after the narrative regarding the events at Caesarea Philippi (8:27–30), Mark presents an account of the Transfiguration. Jesus took his three closest disciples up to a high mountain (Mark 9:2), where God used to meet with the Old Testament heroes of faith, such as Moses (Exod 3:1–2; 19:1–3) and Elijah (1 Kgs 18:17–40; 19:8, 11). On this mountain, Jesus appeared as a heavenly figure (Mark 9:2–3) in conversation with Moses, the giver of the Law, and Elijah, the greatest of the prophets. **Why do Moses and Elijah appear with Jesus?** The text does not say, so any answer is a guess, but a reasonable guess is that together Moses and Elijah represent the Law and the Prophets (= God's entire revelation to his people). When the cloud overshadowed the mountain (9:7; cf. Exod 19:16) and a heavenly voice declared Jesus to be the beloved Son, whose word should be heeded, the implicit claim is that Jesus represents the full and final revelation of God. Needless to say, the disciples could hardly fathom what to make of this event (vv. 5–6, 9–13).

The first verse of Mark's Gospel announces that Jesus Christ (the Messiah) is the Son of God (though some Greek manuscripts omit those last words).[3] Someone familiar with the Old Testament would recognize that "son of God" was a messianic title, not a claim to divinity (see, e.g., 1 Chron 28:6; cf. Exod 4:22). But through the course of the narrative we come to suspect that the title "son of God" as applied to Jesus has a greater significance than when it is applied to Israelite kings. The heavenly voice calls Jesus the "beloved Son" not only at the Transfiguration but also at the baptism (1:9–11), and Jesus addresses God as Father (8:38; 13:32; 14:36). At the crucifixion, the nearby centurion confessed the truth of Mark's first verse (cf. 15:39). Of course, when we read Matthew and Luke, the birth narratives assure us that Jesus is indeed the Son of God in a deeper sense than we might have realized from the title alone (Matt 1:20; Luke 1:35). And we have already seen that John's Gospel exhibits Jesus as the divine son who uniquely reveals the Father (1:18).

Even Jesus's frequent references to himself as "son of man" (Mark 2:10, 28; 9:31; 10:45; etc.) probably alludes to the exalted figure in Daniel's prophecy (Dan 7:13–14), a figure that some prominent Rabbis (such as Rabbi Akiva in the second century) considered to be the davidic messiah and to be enthroned in Daniel 7.[4] It is this title, "son of man," that Jesus uses in his response to the high priest's question as to whether he is "the Christ, the son of the Blessed One" (Mark 14:61). Jesus's first answer, "I am" (v. 62), is provocative but not unique: other people had also claimed to be the Messiah.[5] But the further description of "the son of man sitting at the right hand of power and coming with the clouds of heaven" claims for Jesus divine status, which in turn elicits the charge of "blasphemy" from the high priest (vv. 63–64).[6]

But in Mark 10:18, Jesus seems to deny his own divine status. **What does this verse mean?** We should not understand Mark 10:18 as if Jesus is denying his divinity. Jesus challenges the Rich Young Ruler (RYR) to think through his own assumptions: if the RYR calls Jesus "good," and we all admit that only God is truly good, the RYR should recognize the implications of his own statement—the supreme authority of Jesus (whose word he is about to ignore!).

Even though the Gospels present Jesus as in some ways the embodiment of God (John 14:7–9), they do not present Jesus as identical with God. **How do the Gospels distinguish Jesus from God?** Jesus prays to his Father (Mark 14:36) and he admits ignorance of some information that belongs only to the Father (13:32). In John's Gospel, though Jesus can express identity with the Father (10:30), he also can say, "the Father is greater than I" (14:28). This statement might have reference to Jesus's status while on earth, having been "emptied" (cf. Phil 2:6–8), rather than his eternal status, or it might refer to the eternal relations between Father (begetter) and Son (begotten). Whatever its implications, it clearly differentiates Jesus from the Father.

CONCLUSION

The Gospels present Jesus as the long-awaited Messiah, but they also make clear that he is more than a Messiah—not just David's son, but also David's lord. The way that the Gospels present Jesus as God but also distinguishable from God creates the conundrum that later councils would attempt to work out in their articulations of the doctrine of the Trinity.

DISCUSSION QUESTIONS

1. Read Mark 12:35–37. What point is Jesus trying to make in this passage?
2. Read Mark 1:1–8. This passage quotes Isaiah 40:3 in reference to John the Baptist. In the Isaiah passage, who is the "Lord" whose way will be prepared? When Mark uses the Isaiah passage, to whom does he refer the word "Lord"?
3. Read the account of Jesus's Transfiguration in Mark 9:1–12. What do you regard as the significance of this event? What does it reveal about Jesus?
4. In his trial before the high priest, Jesus provides an answer that elicits a charge of blasphemy from the high priest (Mark 14:61–64). What did Jesus say that so riled the high priest?
5. How do the Gospels present Jesus as different from God? Reflect on Mark 13:32 and John 14:28.

ENDNOTES

1. The reference in John 1:18 depends on which translation you're reading; go online to the NET Bible and see the note on this verse.

2. On the theme of applying to Jesus Old Testament verses

that originally referred to Israel's God (YHWH), see the second chapter in my *The Book of Exodus: Explorations in Christian Theology* Cypress Bible Study Series (Florence, AL: HCU Press, 2020).

3. Again, find online the NET Bible and look at the relevant note to this verse.

4. This is not the normal rabbinic reading, however; see Segal, *Two Powers*, 47–48. This passage from Daniel 7 was rife for speculation on the nature of the divine, as Segal's ch. 2 shows (esp. pp. 47–50).

5. See Wikipedia: "List of Jewish Messiah Claimants."

6. Every sentence in this paragraph is debated by scholars. On Jesus's use of the phrase "son of man" to refer to himself—although a prominent suggestion has been that Jesus uses the phrase to refer to someone else—see Larry W. Hurtado and Paul L. Owen, eds., *Who Is This Son of Man? The Latest Scholarship on a Puzzling Expression of the Historical Jesus* (London: T&T Clark, 2011). On Jesus's response to the high priest in Mark 14:62, see Craig A. Evans, "In What Sense 'Blasphemy'? Jesus before Caiaphas in Mark 14:61–64," in *Jesus and His Contemporaries: Comparative Studies* (Leiden: Brill, 1995). See also Brant Pitre's blog post "Why Is Jesus Accused of Blasphemy in Mark 14?" (Feb. 17, 2016), available online at *The Jesus Blog* (http://historicaljesusresearch.blogspot.com/).

CHAPTER TEN

JESUS AND OUTSIDERS

> Those who are well have no need of a physician, but those who are sick. I came not to call the righteous, but sinners (Mark 2:17).

When I say the name Jesus, what's the first characteristic that comes to mind? Probably near the top of that list would be love and/or compassion. Jesus himself explained that the "new commandment" that he delivered to his disciples was love (John 13:34). But, of course, this commandment is also found in the Old Testament, and Jesus characterized the command to love God (Deut 6:4) and love neighbor (Lev 19:18) as the two greatest commandments, on which the entire Old Testament is based (Matt 22:34–40; cf.

Rom 13:9; etc.). He also encouraged religious leaders to reflect on Hosea 6:6, in which God says, "I desire compassion and not sacrifice" (Matt 9:13; 12:7).

In what ways did Jesus display love or compassion? Jesus's love was displayed fundamentally through the cross, of course, but also in many ways during his ministry. One of the most striking aspects of Jesus's ministry—something that irritated and/or confused many of his contemporaries—was his persistent welcome directed toward "undesirable" people. The Pharisees and scribes were annoyed that "This many receives sinners and eats with them" (Luke 15:2). The crowd was shocked in Jesus's meeting with Zacchaeus that "He has gone to be the guest of a man who is a sinner" (Luke 19:7; cf. Mark 2:14–17). Simon the Pharisee could not believe that this so-called prophet would allow a sinful woman to touch his feet (Luke 7:36–50). When the disciples saw Jesus speaking with the Samaritan woman, "they were amazed that he had been speaking with a woman" (John 4:27). And despite the disciples' best efforts, Jesus insisted on spending some of his busy day with children (Mark 10:13–16).

To what ethnic group was Jesus's ministry primarily directed? Jesus says, "I was sent only to the lost sheep of the house of Israel" (Matt 15:24; cf. 10:5–6). He makes this statement while speaking with a Gentile woman (Syrophoenician, from the district of Tyre and Sidon; 15:21–22) as a justification for not driving a demon out of her daughter. This is an odd scene in which Jesus seems to call this woman a dog (v. 26), though the statement is not so negative as it might seem in our context.[1] We see throughout the Gospels that Jesus does interact primarily with Jews, and all of his disciples are Jewish. But his ministry is ultimately aimed at the whole world (Matt 28:19; Luke 24:47), and he did on occasion encounter and help non-Jews (such as the Syrophoenician woman). Early in Jesus's ministry a Gentile centurion pleaded with Jesus on behalf of his servant (Matt 8:5–13 // Luke 7:1–10), and Jesus readily complied. Jesus made a statement about an end-time banquet in which Gentiles like this centurion would be invited while "the sons of the kingdom" would be excluded (Matt 8:11–12).

The Old Testament had predicted a time in which the Gentiles would be included within God's people. Perhaps most famously, Isaiah had imagined a time when "many peoples will come and say, 'Come, let us go up to the mountain of the Lord'" (2:3), a time when all nations would stream to Zion (v. 2). Isaiah envisioned Egyptians worshipping the Lord (19:19–22). Later in the book, the prophet spoke of foreigners joining themselves to the Lord (56:3–8) so that "My house will be called a house of prayer for all the peoples" (v. 7).

Micah shared these concerns, including identical wording with regard to the nations coming to Zion (Mic 4:1–3 = Isa 2:1–4). In Micah, the vision continues with the Lord declaring that "In that day ... I will assemble the lame and gather the outcasts," and he will make these groups into a strong nation (4:6–7). Zephaniah also prophesied the salvation of the lame and outcasts (3:19). Jesus described his own work in precisely this manner in the Parable of the Banquet (Luke 14:16–24). The banquet would be attended by "the poor and crippled and blind and lame" (v. 21). With these words Jesus echoed the Isaiah passage (Isa 61:1–2) he had read earlier at the synagogue in Nazareth (Luke 4:16–21). This idea drove his entire ministry, since "it is not those who are healthy who need a physician, but those who are sick" (Mark 2:17). In this way (as in so many others), Jesus fulfilled ancient prophecies about what God was preparing for his people.

There were a few times Jesus interacted with Samaritans. **What do you know about Samaritans?** The Bible describes the origins of a syncretic religious group based in northern Israel (2 Kgs 17:25–41), but Samaritans at the time of Jesus could not be described as syncretic. They revered the Torah, and they worshiped only the Israelite God (Yahweh), but they did so on Mt. Gerizim (near Nablus = biblical Shechem), north of Jerusalem. The Samaritan woman asked Jesus about this difference in worship (John 4:20), and Jesus responded essentially by saying that in terms of the proper location of worship, the Jews were right (they worshiped what they knew, and salvation was from them, v. 22), but soon it wouldn't matter (v. 23). The Samaritans were outside proper, biblical religion, and Jesus did not excuse that error, but that did not stop him from reaching out to them, for the purpose of bringing them to proper faith. That was the goal of his (successful) encounter with the Samaritan woman (John 4:28–30, 39–42), as well as his healing of the Samaritan leper (Luke 17:11–19).

The same cause compelled Jesus to attend parties with tax collectors and sinners (Mark 2:15). He did not want sinners to stay in their sinful condition; he came to call the sinners to a better lifestyle, just as a physician does not leave the sick in their sickness (Mark 2:17; cf. John 8:11). Zacchaeus recognized full well that he would not be acceptable to Jesus unless he repented of the sinful practices associated with his tax collecting (Luke 19:8; cf. 3:10–14).

The religious leaders were disgusted that Jesus would so compromise himself among these ungodly people (Luke 15:2; cf. again Mark 2:16; Luke 7:39). In response to this concern, Jesus told some parables, illustrating first the "joy in heaven over one sinner who repents" (15:7, 10, 22–24), but also the unreasonable and unjoyful response to repentance demonstrated sometimes by those who are already "in" (15:25–32; cf. 7:40–50). It is this sort of territorial posture that will cause some of the "sons of the kingdom" to be thrown out of the banquet while Abraham, Isaac, and Jacob host those coming from the east and west (Matt 8:11–12; cf. 21:31–32: tax collectors and prostitutes). (See also the woes in Matt 23.)

CONCLUSION

Jesus's treatment of outsiders with love and compassion was one of the central characteristics of his ministry and one of the prime ways he aggravated religious insiders. This aspect of his life remains a model for all who call themselves followers of Christ.

DISCUSSION QUESTIONS

1. How could it be that tax collectors and prostitutes would enter the kingdom ahead of the religious leaders that Jesus knew? See Matt 21:31–32.
2. What does Jesus's treatment of children display about his character? See Mark 10:13–16. What do we see about the disciples' character in this episode?
3. Why are the disciples amazed at Jesus in John 4:27? What does that fact say about the disciples, and what does it say about Jesus?
4. How does the parable that Jesus told in Luke 7:41–42 address the situation involving Simon the Pharisee? See Luke 7:36–50.
5. How does the Parable of the Banquet (Luke 14:16–24) illustrate the gospel?

ENDNOTES

1. See the helpful blog posts by Larry Hurtado, "Dogs, Doggies, and Exegesis" (Oct. 11, 2012) and "Children & Dogs: More on Mark 7:24–30" (Oct. 12, 2012), both available online at *Larry Hurtado's Blog* (https://larryhurtado.wordpress.com/).

CHAPTER ELEVEN

THE CRUCIFIXION OF JESUS

But we preach Christ crucified, to Jews a stumbling block and to Gentiles foolishness (1 Cor 1:23).

Why did the Romans crucify people? There were much easier ways of killing people. They certainly wanted their crucifixion victims to die, but they also wanted to humiliate them. Crucifixion was typically reserved for political dissidents.[1] According to the second-century historian Appian (*Civil Wars* 1.120), the first-century BC slave rebellion led by Spartacus resulted in the crucifixion of 6000 rebel slaves "along the whole road from Capua to Rome" (115 miles).[2] According to Josephus (*Jewish Antiquities* 17.10.9–10; *Jewish War* 2.5), the Roman general Varus crucified 2000

Jewish rebels after the death of Herod the Great. Sometimes Jewish kings used crucifixion to punish political enemies. Early in the first century BC, Alexander Jannaeus crucified 800 Pharisees because of their opposition to him (Josephus, *Jewish Antiquities* 13.14.2). These examples also show that crucifixion was exceedingly common, that all throughout the Roman Empire, one could see naked men (and the occasional woman) hanging on crosses slowly dying.

Remember that Barabbas was about to be crucified because of his participation in an insurrection (Luke 23:19, discussed in Chapter Five). Probably the same also applies to the two criminals crucified alongside Jesus. These men are called "thieves" in the old KJV (Matt 27:38; Mark 15:27), though in more recent translations the term is often given as "robbers" or even "rebels" (NIV) or "bandits" (NRSV) or "outlaws" (NET).[3] The same Greek word (*lēstēs*) is also used of Barabbas in John 18:40. Since Barabbas is described with this word, and he committed insurrection, it is likely that the two "rebels" crucified beside Jesus were convicted for the same offense, perhaps having participated in the same insurrection.

What was the crime that Jesus was charged with?

Jesus was charged with the same crime as Barabbas at his second trial, the one before Pilate (but not at his first trial, the one before the high priest). The Jewish leaders reported to Pilate that "we found this man misleading our nation and forbidding to pay taxes to Caesar, and saying that he himself is Christ, a king" (Luke 23:2), and Pilate understood them to be accusing Jesus of inciting the people to rebellion (v. 14). If Jesus presented himself as a king, he would pose a threat to Caesar.

But Pilate's questioning as to whether Jesus really did present himself as a king led to confusion (Mark 15:2-5; John 18:33-38). Jesus said he was a king of an otherworldly kingdom (John 18:36), an idea in which Pilate saw no great political threat (John 18:38; Luke 23:4). Nevertheless, pressed by the crowd, Pilate condemned Jesus (Mark 15:15) and posted above his head the charge against him, "The King of the Jews" (Mark 15:26; John 19:19-22).

Why did the Jewish leaders want to dispose of Jesus? The Pharisees early on had wanted to "destroy" Jesus (Mark 3:6) because he did not follow their traditions and he gained a following. Pilate was aware that the Jewish opposition to Jesus stemmed from envy (Mark 15:10). Jesus boldly challenged the authority of the Jewish leaders (Mark 12:12; Matt 23). When Judas agreed to betray him away from the crowds (Mark 14:10-11), they had their chance to discover a charge by which they might accuse him before Pilate. (They had already arrived at the conclusion that he should die, but they had no authority to execute him; for that they needed the Romans [John 18:31].) When the manufactured testimony proved insufficient (Mark 15:53-59), the high priest asked him directly whether he was the Messiah (= a king; v. 61; cf. Luke 23:2). Jesus finally answered in the affirmative, and gave the high priest much more, identifying himself as one "sitting at the right hand of power and coming with the clouds of heaven," at which the high priest cried "blasphemy!"[4]

Of course, Jesus knew exactly what he was doing by challenging the authority of the Jewish leadership, and he knew what the result would be (Mark 8:31; 9:31; 10:33-34). After all, the Son of Man came "to give his life a ransom for many" (Mark 10:45; John 12:27). Still, he did not relish the thought of his crucifixion (Mark 14:36).

Crucifixion was a painful, humiliating death. The Gospels state simply "they crucified him" without further description (Matt 27:35; Mark 15:24; Luke 23:33; John 19:18), but other sources give us some idea of what was involved.[5] Despite the artistic renderings we often see, crucifixion victims were completely nude, the better to humiliate them. They would typically hang there for days; their corpse might then be eaten by birds and dogs. **Why did the Romans not execute people more quickly?** Crucifixion was intended to kill slowly to heap upon the victim maximum shame as a vivid lesson as to what happens to people who defy Rome. The first-century Roman author Seneca recoiled at the physical terror of crucifixion, "wasting away in pain, dying limb by limb, or letting out his life drop by drop" (*Epistle* 101.14). A century earlier, the orator Cicero advised that the word "cross" should "be far removed from not only the bodies of Roman citizens but even from their thoughts, their eyes, and their ears" (*Pro Rabirio* 16).

We can imagine how difficult it must have been for early Christians to convince people that the crucifixion of a Jewish peasant had been instrumental in redeeming humanity from sin. Paul surely knew from experience that this message was perceived as foolishness and a stumbling block (1 Cor 1:23). An ancient drawing (the Alexamenos Graffito; see Wikipedia) depicting the worship of a crucified man with a donkey's head probably intends to mock Christian belief and further illustrates the shame of crucifixion. Not only was the death of the Messiah unexpected (cf. Acts 17:3; and see Chapter Three above), but "even death on a cross" (Phil 2:8) seemingly put him under the curse of God (Gal 3:13). Jesus recognized the shame of the cross, and he despised it (Heb 12:2).

CONCLUSION

If Jesus had come as the military hero that many Jews anticipated in a Messiah (discussed in Chapter Two), the Romans would certainly have wanted to crucify him. Nevertheless, though the Roman governor considered the accusation baseless, he executed Jesus as if he were a rebel leader. Despite the necessary shame inherent in that crucifixion, the cross became central to Christianity, our single boast (Gal 6:14) and single message (1 Cor 2:2).

DISCUSSION QUESTIONS

1. Why did some Jewish leaders want Jesus to die? See Mark 3:6; 12:12.
2. When Jesus stood before the high priest and Sanhedrin, what were these Jewish leaders trying to establish through this trial? See Mark 14:53–65; Luke 22:66–71.
3. What was the charge against Jesus that the Jewish leaders took to Pilate? See Mark 15:1–5; Luke 23:1–16.

4. As for the men hanging beside Jesus, of what crime do you think they had been convicted? Compare different translations of Matthew 27:38; Mark 15:27, and compare the crime of Barabbas (Luke 23:19).

5. If you did not know about crucifixion, how much information about that punishment could you gain from the Gospels? In other words, how much detail to the Gospels provide about what crucifixion entailed? Read Matthew 27:33–54; Mark 15:22–39; Luke 23:33–49; John 19:17–37.

ENDNOTES

1. See, for instance, Larry Hurtado, "Why Was Jesus Crucified?" (Apr. 9, 2009), online at Slate.

2. Wanna see? Go to YouTube and search for "Spartacus (10/10) Movie Clip – Goodbye My Life (1960)."

3. Luke calls them only "criminals" (23:33, 39) and John calls them "men" (19:18).

4. See again note 6 in Chapter Nine.

5. For example, see the unsigned essay "How the Romans Used Crucifixion—Including Jesus's—as a Political Weapon" (Apr. 4, 2015), online at *Newsweek*. Also, listen to the podcast "The Horror of Crucifixion" (Apr. 17, 2011) by New Testament scholar Mark Goodacre, episode 54 at *NT Pod* (podacre.blogspot.com). Or see Wikipedia: "Crucifixion."

CHAPTER TWELVE

THE ACHIEVEMENT OF THE CROSS

> Grace to you and peace from God our Father and the Lord Jesus Christ, who gave Himself for our sins that He might rescue us from this present evil age, according to the will of our God and Father (Gal 1:3–4).

Why did Jesus die? We have examined the death of Jesus from the standpoint of his opponents (Chapter Eleven), why they wanted Jesus to die. But we also see throughout the Gospels that Jesus considered his death to be an essential part of his own ministry. Notice that Mark 8:31 (// Matt 16:21) uses the word *must*: "the Son of Man must ... be killed." **Why did he have to be killed?**

There are several possible answers to that question. (1) According to Jesus, it was necessary "for the Messiah to suffer these things and to enter into his glory" because Scripture had prophesied such things (Luke 24:25-27, 44-47; cf. Acts 17:2-3). (Chapter Three above suggested that Jesus probably had in mind psalms like Psalm 22 and also the "servant" passages in Isaiah.) (2) Jesus gave another reason in John 10:17-18. **What do these verses say about why Jesus died?** The death of Jesus resulted from his own initiative, but Jesus also described it as the Father's will. Remember that in Gethsemane, Jesus prayed that not his own will but the Father's will would be accomplished (Mark 14:36).

Surprisingly, the Gospels do not provide much detail about why the Father willed Jesus to die. The angel tells Joseph that he should name his son Jesus, "for he will save his people from their sins" (Matt 1:21), but the angel does not reveal how Jesus would accomplish this salvation. In speaking about his own death, Jesus usually merely described (predicted) it without interpreting it (Mark 8:31; 9:31; 10:33-34). But at least once he did talk about giving "his life a ransom for many" (Mark 10:45 // Matt 20:28). **What did Jesus mean by that?** Paul mentioned that people have been taken captive by the devil, ensnared by him (2 Tim 2:25-26). Jesus's death would "redeem us from every lawless deed" (Titus 2:14).[1]

John the Baptist declared that Jesus was "the lamb of God who takes away the sin of the world" (John 1:29). **Why did John describe Jesus in this way?** The description might suggest that Jesus would atone for the world's sin just as a lamb would in Israel's sacrificial system (cf. Lev 4:32-35; 5:6). But Jesus's death was also closely associated with Passover (John 19:14), so much so that Paul could even say, "Christ our

Passover also has been sacrificed" (1 Cor 5:7), so perhaps John the Baptist intended for his hearers to think about the Passover lamb commemorating the exodus (cf. Exod 12:1–13). Whatever John may have meant by the phrase "lamb of God," readers of the Gospel usually see this statement as a foreshadowing of Jesus's death as the means by which he would save the world from sin. This idea seems to be connected to the presentation of the suffering servant in Isaiah 53, especially vv. 5–6 and 8.

Also, at the Last Supper, Jesus passed the wine and explained, "this is my blood of the covenant, which is poured out for many for forgiveness of sins" (Matt 26:28). **What does this explanation mean?** The mention of a "new covenant" (Luke 22:20) recalls Jeremiah 31:31 (cf. Heb 8:8–12), where God had promised to "make a new covenant with the house of Israel and with the house of Judah," a covenant in which "I will forgive their iniquity, and their sin I will remember no more" (v. 34). Jeremiah contrasted this covenant with "the covenant which I made with their fathers" at the time of the exodus (v. 32), that is, the covenant at Sinai. This Sinai covenant was instituted with blood: "So Moses took the blood and sprinkled it on the people, and said, 'Behold the blood of the covenant, which the Lord has made with you …" (Exod 24:8). Jesus renewed the covenant with God's people, and he sealed the covenant with the blood of no animal but rather his own (cf. John 1:29). Jesus had to die to establish the new covenant and secure our redemption or ransom from sin.

We have seen in previous chapters that Jesus spent the majority of his time teaching about the kingdom of God and hinting at his own role in establishing that kingdom since he was the Messiah, the King. **What was the role of the Messiah, according to the dominant thought in first-century Judaism?** We have talked a lot (Chapter Two) about how the Messiah was to conquer the enemies of God. **And did Jesus accomplish this part of the Messiah's job?** He did, but not in the anticipated way (Chapter Seven). Instead of battling the Romans or the pagan nations, he battled Satan, demons, disease, sin, and death (= the enemies of God). **How did the crucifixion of Jesus fit into this scheme?** The Gospels represent the crucifixion as the climax of the story, the moment when Jesus achieved his victory and the kingdom was established. It was at this moment that he was clothed in purple and given a crown and acclaimed "King of the Jews" (Mark 15:16–20). Though the Roman soldiers meant these actions to mock and humiliate Jesus, the actions ironically were more appropriate than the soldiers realized. While hanging on the cross, Jesus had above his thorny crown a sign proclaiming him "The King of the Jews" (v. 26), which, again, though intended as an accusation, contained more truth than Pilate knew. Jesus came to establish a kingdom "not of this world" (John 18:36), and that kingdom was established in a manner wholly foreign and unanticipated in this world. This moment of suffering showed Jesus to be truly David's son in the manner of Psalm 22. Jesus had to die in order to conquer his enemies (Ps 110:1) and to establish the kingdom of God.

The New Testament epistles reflect extensively on this aspect of Christ's cross—the victory that it achieved. "For this purpose the Son of God was manifested, that he might destroy the works of the devil" (1 John 3:8). Peter says that Jesus has subjugated "angels and authorities and powers" (1 Pet 3:22). Similarly, Paul says that by means of the cross Jesus "disarmed the rulers and authorities" and "made a public display of them, having triumphed over them" (Col 2:15). According to Paul, "our Savior Jesus Christ … has abolished death" (2 Tim 1:10), and the writer of Hebrews says that Jesus's death destroyed "him who had the power over death, the devil" (Heb 2:14–15). Jesus conquered his enemies through his cross.

CONCLUSION

Why did Jesus die? There are historical reasons having to do with his conflict with the Jewish leaders and the threat he seemed to pose to Roman order. But there are also theological reasons. Jesus died to redeem us from sin, to be a ransom for us. He died to establish the new covenant with God's people, consecrated by his blood. And he died to defeat his enemies and establish his kingdom.

DISCUSSION QUESTIONS

1. Does Jesus explain to his disciples why he will die? After the resurrection, does he explain? What explanations are recorded? See Mark 8:31; 9:31; 10:33–34; Luke 24:25–27, 44–49.
2. What does Jesus mean in Mark 10:45 (// Matt 20:28) that he would give his life as a ransom for

many? What does the context of the passage (Mark 10:41–45) contribute to the meaning of this verse?

3. Do the accounts of the Lord's Supper explain the significance of Jesus's death? See Matthew 26:26–29; Mark 14:22–25; Luke 22:14–23; 1 Corinthians 11:17–34.
4. Read Mark 15. Do you think that Mark intends to present the crucifixion as the coronation of Jesus as the king over his kingdom?
5. In what ways can the crucifixion be considered a moment of victory for Jesus? See Colossians 2:14–15 and Hebrews 2:14–15.

ENDNOTES

1. The word "redeem" in Titus 2:14 (Greek *lutro-ō*) is related to the word "ransom" in Mark 10:45 (*lutron*). See also 1 Pet 3:18–19, where the same word (*lutro-ō*) is used in v. 18 ("redeemed"). Also, Luke 24:21.

CHAPTER THIRTEEN

AT GOD'S RIGHT HAND

Who is to condemn? It is Christ Jesus, who died, yes, who was raised, who is at the right hand of God, who indeed intercedes for us (Rom 8:34).

What is the message of the gospel? It is not merely that Jesus died for our sins, although the death of Jesus is an essential part of the gospel. The most well-known passage where Paul describes what the gospel entails is 1 Corinthians 15:1–5, which uses the word "gospel" (Greek *euangelion*, "good news") in v. 1 and emphasizes the following points: "that Christ died for our sins in accordance with the scriptures, and that he was buried, and that he was raised on the third day in accordance with the scriptures, and that he appeared" to various witnesses, such as Cephas (Peter), the Twelve, and others. The entire chapter is about the resurrection, mostly the resurrection of people, which is entirely dependent on the prior resurrection of Jesus—and not just his death. "If Christ has not been raised, then our proclamation has been in vain and your faith has been in vain" (v. 14). And again: "If Christ has not been raised, your faith is futile and you are still in your sins" (v. 17).

As we saw in Chapter Eleven, all kinds of people died on Roman crosses, and all of them are still dead—except one.

In what ways is the resurrection of Jesus an important element of the gospel? The resurrection not only demonstrates the reality of God's working in Jesus (Rom 1:3–4), but by it Jesus also conquered death (Rev 1:18), and as a result of it Jesus now reigns as king at the right hand of God (Acts 2:33). We may take each of these points in turn.

Does the Bible contain other stories of people rising from the dead? Both Elijah (1 Kgs 17:17–24) and Elisha (2 Kgs 4:32–37) raised young men from the dead by lying atop them. Some random bandit came back to life when his corpse touched the dead bones of Elisha (2 Kgs 13:21). And, of course, Jesus raised Lazarus (John 11) and Jairus's daughter (Mark 5:35–43) and the son of the widow of Nain (Luke 7:11–17). Later, Peter would raise Dorcas/Tabitha (Acts 9:36–43). **What are some differences between the resurrection of Jesus and the resurrection of these others?** First of all, these people were all raised by someone else. In a sense, this is also true regarding the resurrection of Jesus, but the "someone else" in his case was God; "God raised him up" (Acts 2:24). Second, Jesus's body was different from what it had been. Presumably, Lazarus and Jairus's daughter and the others had their regular body after their resurrection, but Jesus's body had transformed somewhat. It was still his physical body; he could be touched (Luke 24:39; John 20:27), and he still had the nail holes (John 20:25), and he ate a fish (Luke 24:42–43). But Luke and John also show that people failed to recognize him (Luke 24:16, 31; John 20:14; 21:4), he had no trouble with locked doors (John 20:19), and he can even vanish while people are staring at him (Luke 24:31).[1]

This odd body possessed by the post-resurrection Jesus is no doubt related to the most important difference between his resurrection and that of others: Jesus is no longer subject to death. Lazarus is now dead, awaiting his final resurrection with all the saints. So, too, is Jairus's daughter and the son of the widow of Nain, and all the others. In this way, the events of the raising of Lazarus and the raising of Jesus are so distinct as to hardly deserve the same name; Lazarus experienced something more like resuscitation, not true resurrection in the Christian sense. And so Paul could call Christ—not Lazarus or any previously raised person—"the first fruits of those who have died" (1 Cor 15:20, 23). "We know that Christ, being raised from the dead, will never die again; death no longer has dominion over him" (Rom 6:9). It is in this way that he "was declared to be the son of God with power according to the spirit of holiness by the resurrection from the dead" (Rom 1:4). Jesus's resurrection —wholly distinct from any resuscitation of a corpse—was a demonstration of his identity, who he claimed to be.

Read Acts 2:22–36. **What was Peter's main point in**

this first gospel sermon? What about Jesus did Peter emphasize? Peter mentioned the death of Jesus (v. 23), but he dwelled on the resurrection. Almost the entire sermon focused on the resurrection, especially interpreting Psalm 16:8–11 in light of this event. Jesus could not be held in death's power (v. 24). **What effect did Jesus's resurrection have on death?** Death is the last enemy that will be destroyed (1 Cor 15:26; Rev 20:11–15), but the destruction of death has already been accomplished through Jesus's resurrection. There are passages in the New Testament that credit the crucifixion with the conquest of death (Jesus conquered death through death; e.g., Heb 2:14; Col 2:15), but it seems that the death of Jesus had the effect of defeating death only because of Jesus's inability to stay dead. The resurrection of Jesus defeated death on our behalf, in that his resurrection guarantees our own resurrection (the main point of 1 Cor 15). "The one who raised the Lord Jesus will raise us also with Jesus" (2 Cor 4:14).

When Peter preached his first gospel sermon in Acts 2, where did he say that Jesus is at that moment? Peter stressed that Jesus ascended to heaven and now reigns as king ("Lord and Messiah," v. 36), sitting at the right hand of God, and he quoted Psalm 110:1 in support of this idea. More than witnesses of his death, the apostles were witnesses of his resurrection and ascension (vv. 32–36; cf. 3:15; 5:32; 10:41; 13:31). The promise of a descendant of David to reign on his throne (2 Sam 7:12–16) has now come to fruition (Acts 2:30).

In Acts 3, Peter and John healed a lame man at the temple,

causing a crowd to form around the men and providing Peter another opportunity to preach. Read Acts 3:11-13. **What was the first thing that Peter wanted to emphasize about Jesus for the crowd at the temple?** God has glorified him. The continuation of the sermon covers the death of Jesus (vv. 14-15, 18) as well as his resurrection (vv. 15, 26) and his exaltation (v. 21). Peter stressed these same points in the next chapter before the Sanhedrin (4:10-11, quoting Ps 118:22), and again in the next chapter, again before the Sanhedrin (5:27-32). Peter spoke this message to Cornelius (10:36-43), and Paul preached it to Jews (13:26-41) and to Gentiles (17:22-31). Their constant message was that Jesus, having been raised from the dead, now reigns as king, sitting at the right hand of God—a theme announced also by Jesus himself (Mark 12:36) and stressed in the apostolic letters (Rom 8:34; 1 Cor 15:25; Eph 1:20; Col 3:1; Heb 1:3, 13; 8:1; 10:12; 12:2; 1 Pet 3:22).

Granted, Paul did say that he "decided to know nothing among you except Jesus Christ, and him crucified" (1 Cor 2:2), but that statement was made in the context of the apostle's desire to stress the perceived weakness and folly of the gospel (see 1:18-31). It was in this same letter that Paul wrote that faith is useless and sins are not forgiven without the resurrection (1 Cor 15:17). So also, when Jesus repeatedly predicted his suffering (Mark 8:31; 9:31; 10:34), he never omitted his resurrection.

The ascension of Jesus is narrated by Luke (Luke 24:50-53; Acts 1:9-11). **Why is the ascension important to us?** The ascension is the moment at which Jesus takes his place on his throne. Without a king there is no kingdom, and Jesus came to establish a kingdom (Mark 1:15). We have seen that the New Testament constantly pictures Jesus as now at the right hand of God, since he has ascended. The whole point of his mission was so that he might become Lord of all (Rom 14:9). Moreover, his current position at God's right hand allows him to do the work of intercession for us (Rom 8:34; Heb 7:25; 1 John 1:1–2).

As Paul said: "Remember Jesus Christ, raised from the dead, a descendant of David [i.e. kingship]—that is my gospel" (2 Tim 2:8). Death, Resurrection, Ascension—that is the gospel. "All authority in heaven and on earth has been given to me" (Matt 28:18) is what Jesus says immediately before commissioning his apostles to tell all nations that there is a new king.[2]

CONCLUSION

If we think the gospel can be summed up with the idea that Jesus died for our sins, we need to pay more attention to the message of the apostles. A death without a resurrection would have produced a vain faith, according to Paul, and the resurrection of Jesus—without the possibility of suffering death again—led to his ascension to the right hand of God, where he now reigns and king and intercedes on our behalf. The faith that we proclaim is a faith that Jesus is Lord and that God raised him from the dead (Rom 10:8–9). Jesus is both Lord and Christ (Acts 2:36). That's good news.

DISCUSSION QUESTIONS

1. How would you summarize the gospel? How does your summary compare to Peter's sermon on the day of Pentecost in Acts 2, or to Paul's summary of the gospel in 1 Cor 15:3–4 or 2 Tim 2:8?
2. Compare Peter's sermons in Acts 2 and Acts 3. What are the common elements? What does Peter want to stress about Jesus in these sermons?
3. What does Paul say about our faith in 1 Corinthians 15:17? What does he mean by that?
4. In Romans 10:8–9, Paul says that salvation is granted to those who believe and confess what? Does this summary of the Christian proclamation cohere with what you have usually heard about the content of saving faith?
5. According to Romans 8:34, where is Christ now and what is he doing?

ENDNOTES

1. It is also Luke and John who narrate stories in which Jesus, during his ministry, strangely escaped detection (Luke 4:30; John 8:59; 10:39), but this characteristic of Jesus seems greatly intensified after his resurrection.

2. My approach to the gospel proclamation of the early church has been influenced by various scholars; see, e.g., C. H. Dodd, *The Apostolic Preaching and Its Developments* (Lon-

don: Hodder and Stoughton, 1936); N. T. Wright, *How God Became King: The Forgotten Story of the Gospels* (New York: HarperCollins, 2012); Matthew W. Bates, *Gospel Allegiance: What Faith in Jesus Misses for Salvation in Christ* (Grand Rapids: Brazos, 2019).

BIBLIOGRAPHY

Appian of Alexandria. Translated by Brian McGing. 6 vols. Loeb Classical Library. Cambridge: Harvard University Press, 2019.

Bates, Matthew W. *Gospel Allegiance: What Faith in Jesus Misses for Salvation in Christ.* Grand Rapids: Brazos, 2019.

Carey, Holly J. *Jesus' Cry from the Cross: Towards a First-Century Understanding of the Intertextual Relationship between Psalm 22 and the Narrative of Mark's Gospel.* London: T&T Clark, 2009.

Dodd, C. H. *The Apostolic Preaching and Its Developments.* London: Hodder and Stoughton, 1936.

Driver, S. R. and Ad. Neubauer. *The Fifty-Third Chapter of Isaiah according to Jewish Interpreters.* Oxford: James Parker, 1877.

Evans, Craig A. "In What Sense 'Blasphemy'? Jesus before

Caiaphas in Mark 14:61–64." Pages 407–434 in *Jesus and His Contemporaries: Comparative Studies*. Leiden: Brill, 1995.

Gallagher, Ed. *The Sermon on the Mount: Explorations in Christian Practice*. Cypress Bible Study Series. Florence, AL: HCU Press, 2021.

_____. *The Book of Exodus: Explorations in Christian Theology*. Cypress Bible Study Series. Florence, AL: HCU Press, 2020.

_____. *The Ekklesia of Christ*. Berean Study Series. Florence, AL: HCU Press, 2015.

Hurtado, Larry W., and Paul L. Owen, eds., *Who Is This Son of Man? The Latest Scholarship on a Puzzling Expression of the Historical Jesus*. London: T&T Clark, 2011.

Josephus. Translated by Henry St. J. Thackeray et al. 10 vols. Loeb Classical Library. Cambridge: Harvard University Press, 1926–1965.

Segal, Alan F. *Two Powers in Heaven: Early Rabbinic Reports about Christianity and Gnosticism*. Boston, MA: Brill, 1977.

Wood, Bryant G. Wood. "Hittites and Hethites: A Proposed Solution to an Etymological Conundrum." *Journal of the Evangelical Theological Society* 54 (2011): 239–50.

Wright, N. T. *How God Became King: The Forgotten Story of the Gospels*. New York: HarperCollins, 2012.

Scripture Index

Old Testament

Genesis

3:14–19	6
3:15	3, 6
4:24	28
5:1	26
6:9	26
10:1	26
11:27	26
38	26
38:13–15	27
38:24–26	27
49:9–12	7n

Exodus

3:1–2	60
4:22	29, 61
12:1–13	79
19:1–3	60
19:16	60
20:4–11	60
24:8	79

Leviticus

4:3	2
4:5	2
4:16	2
4:32–35	78
5:6	78
6:22	2
8:12	2
19:18	65

Numbers

24:17	7n

Deuteronomy

6:4	65
6:13	47
6:16	47
7:22	5
8:3	47
30:1–5	16

Joshua

2	26
2:1	27
6:25	26

Ruth

1:4	26
3	27
4:10	26
4:13	26

1 Samuel

2:10	6n

2:35	6n	5:6–10	41
8:7	38	5:14	28
10:1	2	7	28
12:3	6n	7:12–16	3, 6, 9, 10, 86
12:5	6n	7:12–17	4
13:13–14	4	7:15	4
13:14	9	8	10
15:11	4	8:1–13	41
16	4	8:2	10
16:6	6n	11	27
16:13	2	11:3	26
16:23	10	11:14–17	10
17	10, 16	13:14	10
17:34–36	10	19:21	6n
17:51	10, 41	22:51	6n
17:54	10	23:1	6n
17:57	10	23:34	26
18:5–7	10	**1 Kings**	
18:7	40	6	4
24:6	6n	11:9–13	4
24:10	6n	17:17–24	84
26:9	6n	18:17–40	60
26:11	6n	19:8	60
26:16	6n	19:11	60
26:23	6n	19:16	2
2 Samuel		**2 Kings**	
1:14	6n	4:32–37	84
1:16	6n	8:19	4
3:1	41		

13:21	84	22	22, 23, 78, 80
17:25–41	68	28:8	6n
25:7	5	65:7	60 |//

13:21	84
17:25–41	68
25:7	5

1 Chronicles

16:22	2
22:8	10
22:10	4, 6, 29
28:3	10
28:6	4, 6, 29, 61

2 Chronicles

6:42	6n

Job

38:8–11	60

Psalms

2	4, 10
2:2	6n
2:8–9	8, 46
2:9	11
3	22
4	22
5	22
16	22
16:8–11	22, 86
16:10	22
18:50	6n
20:6	6n
22	22, 23, 78, 80
28:8	6n
65:7	60
84:9	6n
89:3–4	4
89:9	60
89:20–37	4
89:38	6n
89:38–51	5
89:51	6n
96:10	35
97:1	35, 38
98:6	38
105:15	2
107:29	60
110:1	3, 6, 50, 58, 80
118:22	56, 87
132	4
132:10	6n
132:17	6n

Isaiah

1:1	4
2:1–4	5, 67
2:2	67
2:2–4	16
2:3	67
7:1	4

11	10
11:1	4
11:1–10	4, 17, 23
11:2	16
11:4	10, 29, 46, 55
11:6–9	4
11:10	5
19:19–22	67
40:3	59, 63
45:1	6n
53	21, 23, 40
53:5–6	79
53:6	21
53:7–9	21
53:8	79
53:10–11	21
53:11–12	21
53:12	21
56:3–8	67
56:7	67
61:1–2	68

Jeremiah

23:5	1
23:5–6	5
30:8–10	17
31:31	79
31:32	79
31:34	79
33:14–17	5

Lamentations

4:20	6n

Ezekiel

34:23–24	5
37:15–28	17, 35
37:21–24	5, 16
37:24	16
37:24–25	

Daniel

2	11, 17, 36
2:31–34	11
2:34–35	11, 36
2:38	11
2:44	11, 38
7	61, 64n
7:13–14	61
9:25–26	2

Hosea

2:18	5
6:6	54, 66

Amos

9:11–15	5

Micah

4:1–3	5, 67
4:6–7	67
5:2	29

Habakkuk

3:13   6n

Zephaniah

3:19   67

Zechariah

12:7–8   5
12:10   5
13:1   5

New Testament

Matthew

1:1   6, 9, 16, 39n, 58
1:1–17   30
1:2–16   31
1:2–17   26
1:3   26
1:5   26
1:6   26
1:16   39n
1:17   39n
1:18   39n
1:18–25   30
1:20   3, 29, 61
1:21   49, 51, 78
1:23   29
2:2   29
2:4   29
2:6   29
2:16   29
3   39
3:2   37
4:1   47
4:1–11   47, 51
4:8–9   50
4:17   36, 37, 39, 53
4:23   52
4:24–25   38
5–7   57
5:3   37, 57
5:3–12   53
5:9   41
5:10   37
5:17–48   43
5:19–20   37
5:21–26   53
5:27–30   49, 53
5:38–48   49, 53
5:39   41
5:41   41
5:44   41
6:1–18   54
6:19–24   54
6:25–34   49, 54

7:1–6	54	13:24–30	55
7:12	54	13:31	37
7:21	37	13:33	37
7:28	57n	13:36–43	55
7:28–29	43, 52, 57	13:44	37
8:5–6	43, 48	13:44–50	55
8:5–13	67, 69	13:45	37
8:11–12	37, 67	13:47	37
8:16	39	13:53	57n
8:17	21	13:54	52
8:19	52	15:1–14	42
9:13	54, 66	15:2	54
9:27	3	15:3–4	54
9:35	37, 39, 52	15:21–22	66
10:5–6	66	15:22	3
10:7	37, 39	15:24	66
11:1	57n	15:26	66
11:2	39n	16:13–20	19, 58
11:19	43–44	16:13–23	1, 6, 8
12:7	66	16:16	29, 39n
12:22–24	39, 44	16:20	39n
12:22–29	51	16:21	19, 77
12:23	3	16:24	41
12:28	36–37, 39, 48	16:24–26	55
		16:28	37
12:38	52	17:22–23	1
13:10–17	57	18:1–4	44
13:22	49	18:3–4	37
13:24	37	18:22	28

18:23	37	26:31–35	1
19:1	57n	26:56	1
19:12	37	26:63–64	39n
19:14	36–37	26:69–75	1
19:23	37	27:17	39n
19:24	36	27:22	39n
20:1	37	27:33–54	76
20:17–19	1	27:35	74
20:28	78, 81	27:38	72, 76
20:30–31	3	28:18	38, 88
21:9	3	28:19	67
21:15	3	**Mark**	
21:23	52	1:1	39n, 59
21:31	36–37	1:1–8	63
21:31–32	69–70	1:9–11	61
21:43	36–37	1:12–13	47
22:2	37	1:15	9, 36, 53, 57, 88
22:29	54	1:21–27	47
22:33	52, 57	1:21–28	39
22:34–40	65	1:24	47, 60
22:41–46	3, 6	1:24–25	42, 45
23	69, 73	1:26	48
23:2–4	42	1:27	43, 53
23:16	42	1:27–28	39
25:1	37	1:32–33	42, 45
25:31–46	44	1:32–34	43, 48
26:1	57n	1:40	45n, 48
26:26–29	82	1:44	41, 45
26:28	49, 51, 79		

2:1–2	52	4:38	52
2:1–12	48–49, 51	4:39–41	60
2:1–3:6	45	4:41	43, 58
2:3–4	43	5:1–20	39, 47
2:5	60	5:3	48
2:7	60	5:4	48
2:10	60–61	5:5	48
2:13	52	5:7	47, 60
2:14–17	66	5:12	42, 47
2:15	68	5:19–20	42, 45
2:15–17	43	5:22–23	43, 48
2:16	69	5:25–27	48
2:17	65, 68–69	5:25–28	45n
2:28	43, 60–61	5:30–31	19
3:6	73, 75	5:35–43	84
3:11	60	5:43	42, 45
3:12	42, 45	6:6	52
3:13–19	38	6:7	48
3:14–15	48	6:13	48
3:22–30	48	6:14–15	43
3:27	48	6:37	19
4	54	6:52	59
4:10–12	19, 42, 57	6:53–57	45n
4:11	39n	7:1–23	45
4:11–12	54, 59	7:14–19	19
4:15	49	7:24–26	43
4:26	39n	7:24–30	48
4:30	39n	7:32	45, 48
4:33–34	54, 57	7:36	42

7:37	43	9:17–29	48
8:11–13	42, 45	9:18	48
8:14–21	19, 59	9:30–32	20, 23
8:18	59	9:31	61, 73, 78, 81, 87
8:22	45, 48		
8:26	42	9:33–37	20
8:27–28	43	9:38	48
8:27–30	19, 58–60	9:47	39n
8:29	39n, 43, 45, 59	10:1–12	43
		10:13–16	66, 70
8:30	42, 45	10:14	37
8:31	59, 73, 77–78, 81, 87	10:14–15	39n
		10:17–31	43
8:31–32	19	10:18	62
8:32	59	10:23–25	39n
8:33	19	10:32–34	20
8:34	20	10:33–34	73, 77, 81
8:38	61	10:34	87
9:1	39n	10:35–40	20
9:1–12	63	10:41–45	82
9:2	60	10:44	59
9:2–3	60	10:45	61, 74, 78, 81, 82n
9:5–6	60		
9:7	60	10:46–52	45n, 48, 57
9:9	42		
9:9–13	60	11:10	39n
9:14–29	39	11:18	52
9:17	48	12:1–11	55, 57
9:17–18	43	12:10–11	56

12:12	55, 57, 73, 75
12:34	39n
12:35–37	43, 58, 63
12:36	50, 87
12:41–44	43
13:18–27	43
13:32	61–63
14:10–11	73
14:21	21
14:22–25	20, 82
14:25	39n
14:31	9
14:36	61–62, 74, 78
14:48–49	21
14:53–56	75
14:61	61
14:61–62	39n, 58
14:61–64	63
14:62	61, 64n
14:63–64	61
15	23, 82
15:1–5	75
15:2–5	73
15:7	35
15:10	73
15:15	73
15:16–20	80
15:17	38
15:22–39	76
15:24	74
15:26	38, 73, 80
15:27	72, 76
15:34	22
15:39	61
15:43	39n
15:53–59	73
15:61	73

Luke

1:26–38	30
1:27	28
1:32	58
1:32–33	25, 28
1:35	28, 29, 61
1:46–55	29
1:53	29
1:69	28
1:69–79	29, 50
1:71	29
1:74	29, 46
1:77	49
2:4	28
2:11	28, 39n
2:26	39n
3:3	49
3:7–18	53
3:10–14	69

3:23–38	27, 30–31	15:10	69
4:1–13	47	15:22–24	69
4:16–21	68	15:25–32	69
4:30	89n	16:16	36
4:41	39n	16:19–31	56
5:3	52	17:11–19	68
5:17	52	17:20–21	34, 55
7:1–10	67	17:21	37
7:11–17	84	19:1–10	43
7:36–50	43, 66, 70	19:7	66
7:39	69	19:8	69
7:40	52	22:14–23	82
7:40–50	69	22:20	79
7:41–42	70	22:24	20
7:47–49	49	22:30	38
9:18–23	19	22:33	9
9:20	39n	22:37	21
9:60	37	22:49–50	9
10:9	37	22:66–71	75
10:17–18	48	23:1–16	75
10:19	48	23:2	39n, 72–73
10:30–37	43	23:4	73
11:20	39	23:5	52–53
13:11	49	23:14	72
13:16	49, 51	23:19	35, 72, 76
14:16–24	44, 67, 70	23:33	74, 76n
14:21	68	23:33–49	76
15:2	66, 69	23:39	76n
15:7	69	24:16	85

24:18	20	4:22	68
24:19–24	20	4:23	68
24:21	16, 82n	4:27	66, 70
24:25–26	18, 23	4:28–30	68
24:25–27	20, 78, 81	4:39–42	68
24:26	39n	4:46–47	48
24:31	85	5:18	59
24:39	85	6:14	43
24:42–43	85	7:20	44
24:44–47	78	7:25–31	43, 45
24:44–48	21	7:28	52
24:44–49	81	7:40	43
24:47	67	7:41–44	43, 45
24:50–53	87	8:11	69

John

1:1	59	8:44	47
1:1–18	59	8:48	40, 44
1:14	25	8:48–52	39, 44
1:17	39n	8:58	59
1:18	59, 61, 63n	8:59	89n
1:29	78–79	9:1–3	49
1:38	52	9:17	43
1:41	39n, 43, 45	10:17–18	78
3:2	52	10:20–21	44
3:3	37	10:30	59, 62
3:5		10:39	89n
4	43	11	84
4:19	43	11:27	39n
4:20	68	11:28	52
		12:27	74

12:31	47	21:4	85
12:38	21	**Acts**	
13:2	47, 49	1:9–11	87
13:27	47	2	86, 89
13:34	65	2:22–36	85
14:7–9	62	2:23	85
14:28	62–63	2:24	50–51, 84, 86
14:30	47	2:25–28	22
16:11	47	2:30	86
17:3	39n	2:32–36	86
18:10	9, 41	2:33	84
18:31	73	2:36	86, 88
18:33–38	73	3	86, 89
18:36	37–38, 41, 47, 73, 80	3:11–13	87
18:38	73	3:14–15	87
18:40	72	3:15	86–87
19:14	78	3:18	21, 87
19:17–37	76	3:21	87
19:18	74, 76n	3:26	87
19:19–22	73	4:10–11	87
19:24	22	5:27–32	87
20:14	85	5:32	86
20:16	52	8:32–35	21
20:19	85	9:36–43	84
20:25	85	10:36–43	87
20:27	85	10:38	49, 51
20:28	59	10:41	86
20:31	39n	13:22	9

13:26–41	87	15:17	84, 87, 89
13:31	86	15:20	85
13:35	22	15:23	85
16	22	15:25	87
17:2–3	21, 78	15:26	50, 86
17:3	75		
17:22–31	87		
19:13–17	48		

2 Corinthians

4:14	86

Romans

1:3–4	84
1:4	85
6:9	85
8:34	83, 87–89
10:8–9	88–89
13:9	66
14:9	xiii, 88
14:10	xiii

Galatians

1:3–4	77
3:13	75
6:14	75

Ephesians

1:20	87
6:12	47

Philippians

2:6–8	62
2:8	75

1 Corinthians

1:18–31	87
1:23	71, 74
2:2	75, 87
5:7	79
11:17–34	82
15	86
15:1	83
15:1–5	83
15:3	21
15:3–4	89
15:14	84

Colossians

2:14–15	82
2:15	81, 86
3:1	87

2 Timothy

1:10	81
2:8	88–89
2:25–26	78

Titus

2:14	78, 82n

Hebrews

1:3	87
1:13	87
2:14	50–51, 86
2:14–15	81–82
7:25	88
8:1	87
8:8–12	79
10:12	87
12:2	75, 87

1 Peter

3:18	82n
3:18–19	82n
3:22	81, 87

1 John

1:1–2	88
3:8	81

Revelation

1:18	84
20:11–15	86

ALSO BY ED GALLAGHER

Hebrew Scripture in Patristic Biblical Theory (Brill, 2012)

The Biblical Canon Lists from Early Christianity (Oxford, 2017)
with John D. Meade

The Book of Exodus (HCU Press, 2019)

The Sermon on the Mount (HCU Press, 2020)

Berean Study Series edited by Ed Gallagher

(HCU Press)

www.ingramcontent.com/pod-product-compliance
Lightning Source LLC
LaVergne TN
LVHW091558060526
838200LV00036B/903